DK EYEWITNESS TOP 10 TRAVEL GUIDES

MIAMI
AND THE KEYS

JEFFREY KENNEDY

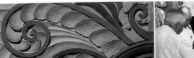

Left **Deco District** Right **Domino players, Little Havana**

DK

LONDON, NEW YORK,
MELBOURNE, MUNICH AND DELHI
www.dk.com

Produced by Blue Island Publishing
Reproduced by Colourscan, Singapore
Printed and bound by South China
Printing Co. Ltd, China

First published in Great Britain in 2003
by Dorling Kindersley Limited
80 Strand, London WC2R 0RL
A Penguin Company

**Reprinted with revisions 2005, 2007
Copyright 2003, 2007 ©
Dorling Kindersley Limited, London**

Contents

Miami's Top 10

SoBe Life   8
Deco District   10
Calle Ocho, Little Havana   14
Villa Vizcaya   16
Merrick's Coral Gables
Fantasies   18
Lowe Art Museum   20
The Wolfsonian   22
Gold Coast Highway A1A   24
Key West   26
The Everglades   28
Beach Resorts   30
Snorkeling and Diving   32
Sports Activities   34
Parks, Gardens, and Zoos   36
Lively Arts   38
Festivals   40
Museums   4
Historic Sites and
Monuments   4
Architectural Wonders   4
Offbeat Places   4

A CIP catalogue record is available from
the British Library.

ISBN: 978-1-40531-933-1

Within each Top 10 list in this book, no
hierarchy of quality or popularity is
implied. All 10 are, in the editor's
opinion, of roughly equal merit.

In this book, floors are referred to in
accordance with American usage, i.e.,
the "first floor" is at ground level.

Cover – **Alamy Images**: Robert Harding World Imagery main; **Corbis**: Joseph Sohm cl; **DK Images**: Linda
Whitwam bl. Spine – **DK Images**: Steve Guyapy. Back – **DK Images**: Max Alexander tc, tr; Peter Wilson tl.

Left **Downtown Miami** Right **Beach, Fort Lauderdale**

Spots for
People-Watching   50
Gay and Lesbian Venues   52
Chic Shopping Centers   54
Malls and Markets   56
Nightlife   58
Restaurants   60
Drives and Walks   62
Romantic Spots   64
Children's Attractions   66

Around Miami and the Keys

Miami Beach and
Key Biscayne   70
Downtown and Little
Havana   82
North of Downtown   90
Coral Gables and
Coconut Grove   98
South of Coconut Grove   106

The Keys   114
Side Trips   126

Streetsmart
Planning Your Trip   134
Sources of Information   135
Tips for Arriving
in Miami   136
Tips for Getting
Around Miami   137
Media Sources   138
Ways to Stay Healthy
and Safe   139
Things to Avoid   140
Money and
Communications Tips   141
Ways to Save Money   142
Senior and Disabled
Travelers   143
Accommodation Tips   145
Places to Stay   146

Left **Alley off Worth Avenue, Palm Beach** Right **Biltmore Hotel, Coral Gables**

Key to abbreviations
Adm admission charge payable **Free** no admission charge

3

MIAMI'S
TOP 10

SoBe Life
8–9

Deco District
10–13

Calle Ocho, Little Havana
14–15

Villa Vizcaya
16–17

Merrick's Coral Gables
Fantasies
18–19

Lowe Art Museum
20–21

The Wolfsonian
22–23

Gold Coast Highway A1A
24–25

Key West
26–27

The Everglades
28–29

Top 10 of Everything
30–67

MIAMI'S TOP 10

Highlights of Miami

At its best, Miami is all pastel hues and warm, velvety zephyrs – a tropical reverie. The culture is sensuous and physical, often spiked with Caribbean rhythms and accents. Outdoor activities hold sway throughout the area, at the world-famous beaches and in the turquoise waters; the vibrant nightlife, too, attracts pleasure-seekers, while significant historical sights are around every corner.

Sunrise
Carol City
Miami
10 Kendall
9

1 SoBe Life
Ever since *Miami Vice* *(see p72)* drew attention to this fun-zone, hedonists have flocked for the beaches and nightlife *(see pp8–9)*.

2 Deco District
The whimsical architecture on South Beach ultimately traces its roots back to 1920s Paris *(see p13)*, but it underwent fruitful, exotic influences along the way and blossomed into Florida's own Tropical Deco *(see pp10–13)*.

3 Calle Ocho, Little Havana
The Cubanization of Miami changed it from sleepy resort to dynamic megalopolis. Little Havana fuels the impression that Miami is Latin American at heart *(see pp14–15)*.

Tamiami
Westwood
Kendale Lakes
94
Lindgren Acres
Ric
South Miami Heigh
Goulc

4 Villa Vizcaya
One immensely rich man's aspiration to European grandeur and appreciation of Western artistic heritage led to the creation of what is probably Miami's most beautiful cultural treasure *(see pp16–17)*.

5 Merrick's Coral Gables Fantasies
The 1920s boom saw a need to build not only structures but also an identity. George Merrick rose to the challenge and created fantasy wonderlands that continue to stir the imagination today *(see pp18–19)*.

Previous pages **Marlin Hotel, South Beach**

Lowe Art Museum
6 This major art museum, created by an endowment from George Merrick, has around 12,000 works of art, including masterpieces from cultures the world over, and from every age *(see pp20–21)*.

The Wolfsonian
7 This superb museum (which began life as a storage company) owes much to its founder's passion for collecting 20th-century propaganda art and design artifacts of the period 1885–1945 *(see pp22–3)*.

Gold Coast Highway A1A
8 Route A1A hugs the sands of the Gold Coast, wending through Florida's wealthiest and most beautiful areas *(see pp24–5)*.

Key West
9 This mythic isle lives up to its reputation as the most outlandishly free spot in the US. A frothy mix of maritime traditions and laid-back style *(see pp26–7)*.

The Everglades
10 Taking up most of South Florida, the Everglades is a vast sea of swamp and sawgrass, dotted with subtropical forests and populated with prolific wildlife. It is also home to Native American Seminoles and Miccosukees *(see pp28–9 & p41)*.

SoBe Life

The nickname for Miami's beautiful South Beach was inspired by Manhattan's SoHo, and it's become every bit as fashionable and hip as its New York counterpart. Now the "American Riviera" is an ebullient mix of beach life, club-crawling, lounge-lizarding, and alternative chic, attracting devotees from around the globe. Yet, SoBe's modern posh character is also nicely blended with just the right amount of tacky kitsch and downright sleaze.

1 Ocean Drive

Strolling, skating, or biking along this beachfront strip is the way the locals do it. From about 6th Street and north, take in the toned, tanned athletes, the abundant, ice-cream-colored Art Deco architecture *(see pp10–13)*, and the people-watching cafés.

News Café

⏱ Parking is a problem everywhere along here, so once you find a place, leave the car and walk. Be aware that you'll need to feed the meter a feast of coins, unless you choose one of the parking garages.

🍴 To participate fully in the SoBe experience, the News Café should definitely be your choice for eats.

Map R–S 3–6

Top 10 Attractions

1. Ocean Drive
2. Lummus Park Beach
3. News Café
4. Casa Casuarina
5. Marlin Hotel Bar
6. Collins and Washington Avenues
7. Old City Hall
8. Española Way
9. Lincoln Road Mall
10. SoBe Clubs

2 Lummus Park Beach

This swath of busy park and 300-ft (90-m) wide beach *(below)* stretches for ten blocks, from 5th St north. Much of the immaculate sand was imported.

3 News Café

The café-restaurant at 800 Ocean Drive continues to be action central for So-Be social life. Sit and read the morning paper, available in several languages, over a full breakfast – or just watch the action.

Beach Patrol Headquarters

4 Casa Casuarina

1114 Ocean Drive (not open to the public) was bought by fashion designer Gianni Versace in 1993 for $3.7 million. He was gunned down on its steps in 1997. The Mediterranean-Revival style building was formerly called Amsterdam Palace.

5 Marlin Hotel Bar

The sparkling hotel at 1200 Collins Avenue *(right)* sports one of SoBe's best places to while away the time with locals. The décor is the apotheosis of the chrome aesthetic – everything seems to be made of curving aluminum.

For the Deco District See pp10–13

6 Collins and Washington Avenues

These scruffier, funkier cousins of Ocean Drive offer kinky shops and top nightclubs, but also some fine Art Deco buildings of their own, including the Miami Beach Post Office.

7 Old City Hall

The 1920s Mediterranean-Revival, buff-colored tower *(left)* is a distinctive South Beach landmark. Its red-tile roof can be seen for blocks around. The building is now a courthouse.

8 Española Way

Between 14th and 15th streets, and Washington and Drexel avenues, Española Way is a Mediterranean-Revival enclave that is all salmon-colored stucco, stripy awnings, and red-tile roofs. It now houses boutiques and offbeat art galleries. Built in 1922–5, it was meant to be an artists' colony but instead became an infamous red-light district at one stage of its history.

9 Lincoln Road Mall

Built in the 1920s as an upscale shopping district, it became one of the country's first pedestrian malls in the '60s. Its current incarnation with art studios and galleries is the brainchild of the South Florida Art Center.

10 SoBe Clubs

Most of South Beach's top clubs are located on Washington and Collins avenues, between 5th and 16th streets. Few get going until at least midnight. Choose between straight, gay and mixed venues *(see pp76–7)*.

Gay Renaissance

South Beach is now world famous as a top gay vacation destination. It is estimated that up to half of the Deco District apartments are gay-occupied. Rainbow flags are everywhere you look, indicating gay-friendly businesses. Gay festivals attract thousands from around the world, flocking to the all-night raves and beach parties. A culture of the Body Beautiful thrives here, which, combined with the constant ebb and flow of revelers, makes the area a vast playground for the sexually various. Gay people now enjoy considerable political clout, both locally and statewide.

For more on SoBe's nightlife See pp58–9

9

Deco District

SoBe's Art Deco District consists of some 800 preserved buildings, the cream of them along Ocean Drive. This splendid array of structures embodies Miami's unique interpretation of the Art Deco style, which took the world by storm in the 1920s and '30s. Florida's take on it is often called Tropical Deco (see pp12–13), which befits the fun-and-sun approach to life. Often hotels were made to look like ocean liners (Nautical Moderne) or given the iconography of speed (Streamline Moderne).

Park Central

🕙 Guided tours are held on Wednesdays, Thursdays, Fridays, Saturdays, and Sundays. Otherwise, a self-guided audio tour can be rented from the Art Deco Welcome Center.

🍽 Mango's Tropical Café, at 900 Ocean Drive, lives up to everything its name might imply – florid and steamy, and always very happening.

Map R–S 3–4
• Miami Design Preservation League and Art Deco Welcome Center, 1001 Ocean Drive at 10th, in the Oceanfront Auditorium (305-531-3484)
• 11am–4pm daily

Top 10 Buildings

1. Park Central
2. Beacon Hotel
3. Colony Hotel
4. Waldorf Towers
5. Breakwater Hotel
6. Beach Patrol Stations
7. Clevelander Hotel
8. Leslie Hotel
9. Cardozo Hotel
10. Cavalier Hotel

Park Central
1 A 1937 favorite by Henry Hohauser, the most famous architect in Miami at the time. Here he used the nautical theme to great effect.

Beacon Hotel
2 The abstract decoration above the ground floor of the Beacon has been brightened by a contemporary color scheme, an example of "Deco Dazzle," introduced by designer Leonard Horowitz in the 1980s.

Colony Hotel
3 Perhaps the most famous of the Deco hotels along here, primarily because its stunning blue neon sign *(left)* has featured in so many movies and TV series.

Waldorf Towers
4 Here is one of the first examples (1937) of Nautical Moderne, where the style is carried to one of its logical extremes with the famous ornamental lighthouse on the hotel's roof. Fantasy towers were the stock in trade for Deco architects.

5 Breakwater Hotel
The classic Streamline Moderne hotel *(left)* was built in 1939. It features blue and white "racing stripes," which give the impression of speed, and a striking central tower that recalls both a ship's funnel and Native-American totems.

6 Beach Patrol Stations
Even the lifeguard stations are done up in Deco on South Beach. Looking perhaps more like a homemade flying saucer that has just landed on the beach, these pink and yellow follies embody the spirit of fun that pervades the lifestyle.

South Beach (SoBe)

7 Clevelander Hotel
Albert Anis used classic Deco materials – especially the glass blocks in the hotel's bar, which is now a top South Beach neon-lit nightspot. Typical Deco features include vertical fluting, geometric decorative touches, the "eyebrow" overhangs shading the windows, and the stripy lettering on the sign.

8 Leslie Hotel
The Leslie (1937) is cockatoo-colored, white and yellow with gray accents *(below)* – a color scheme typical of those currently in favor along Ocean Drive. Originally, however, Deco coloring was quite plain, usually white with only the trim in colors. Nor were the backs of the buildings painted, since money was too tight in the 1930s to allow anything more than a jazzy façade. The Leslie's interior has recently been renovated.

9 Cardozo Hotel
A late Hohauser work (1939) and the favorite of Barbara Capitman *(see p13)*, this is a Streamline masterpiece, in which the detail of traditional Art Deco is replaced with beautifully rounded sides, aerodynamic racing stripes, and other expressions of the modern age. The terrazzo floor utilizes this cheap version of marble to stylish effect. It was reopened in 1982 and is now owned by singer Gloria Estefan.

10 Cavalier Hotel
A traditional Art Deco hotel *(left)*, which provides quite a contrast to the later Cardozo next door. Where the Cardozo emphasizes the horizontal and vaguely nautical, this façade is starkly vertical and temple-like. The temple theme is enhanced by beautifully ornate vertical stucco friezes, which recall the abstract, serpentine geometric designs of the Aztecs and other Meso-American cultures.

For details about staying at SoBe's Art Deco hotels See p147

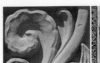

Striking motifs on Tropical Deco buildings

Tropical Deco Features

1 Tropical Motifs
These include Florida palms and panthers, orchids and alligators, but especially birds, such as flamingos and cranes.

2 Ice-Cream Colors
Actually, most Deco buildings here were originally white, with a bit of painted trim; the present-day rich pastel palette "Deco Dazzle" was the innovation of Miami designer and Capitman collaborator Leonard Horowitz in the 1980s.

3 Nautical Features
What better way to remind visitors of the ocean and its pleasures than with portholes and ship-railings? Some of the buildings resemble beached liners.

4 Curves and Lines
This suggestion of speed is the essence of the Streamline Moderne style – it is an implicit appreciation of the power of technology.

5 Stucco Bas-Relief Friezes
These sculptural bands offered designers endless possibilities for a wonderful mix of ancient and modern motifs and themes.

6 Stylized, Geometric Patterning
This was a nod to the extreme modernity of Cubism, as well as, again, the power and precision of technology, espoused by Bauhaus precepts.

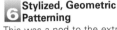

Sunburst motif, Cardozo

7 Fantasy Towers
Many Deco buildings try to give the viewer a sense of something mythical – towers that speak of far shores or exalted visions – and that effectively announce the hotel's name, as well.

8 Neon
Used mostly for outlining architectural elements, neon lighting, in a glamorous range of colors, came into its own with Tropical Deco.

9 Chrome
What touch more perfectly says "modern" than a cool, incorruptible silver streak? Chrome is used as detailing on and within many buildings.

10 Glass Blocks
Used in the construction of many Deco walls, the glass blocks give a sense of light and lightness in a part of the country where indoor-outdoor living is year-round.

"Aztec" frieze, Cavalier

For other architectural wonders in and around Miami See pp46–7

Top 10 Architects

1. **Henry Hohauser** Park Central, Colony, Edison, Cardozo, Governor, Essex, Webster, Century, Taft
2. **Albert Anis** Clevelander, Waldorf, Avalon, Majestic, Abbey, Berkeley Shore, Olympic
3. **Anton Skislewicz** Breakwater, Kenmore
4. **L. Murray Dixon** Tiffany, Palmer House, Fairmont, Tudor, Senator, St. Moritz
5. **Igor B. Polevitsky** Shelborne
6. **Roy F. France** Cavalier
7. **Robert Swartburg** Delano, The Marseilles
8. **Kichnell & Elliot** Carlyle
9. **Henry O. Nelson** Beacon
10. **Russell Pancoast** Bass Museum

Deco Dazzle
In the 1980s, some 150 buildings were colored by Leonard Horowitz, to the dismay of purists.

The Story of Tropical Deco

The Art Deco style took the world stage following the 1925 Exposition in Paris, synthesizing all sorts of influences, from Art Nouveau's flowery forms, Bauhaus, and Egyptian imagery to the geometric patterns of Cubism. In 1930s America, Art Deco buildings reflected the belief that technology was the way forward, absorbing the speed and edginess of

Streamline Moderne

the Machine Age as well as the fantasies of science fiction and even a tinge of ancient mysticism. The thrilling new style was just what was needed to counteract the gloom of the Great Depression and give Americans a coherent vision for the future. In Miami, the style was exuberantly embraced and embellished upon with the addition of numerous local motifs, becoming "Tropical Deco." Its initial glory days were not to last long, however. Many hotels became soldiers' barracks in World War II and were torn down afterward. Fortunately, Barbara Baer Capitman fought a famous battle to preserve the buildings. The Miami Beach Historic District was designated in 1979.

13

Calle Ocho, Little Havana

Cubans live all over South Florida, but Little Havana has been their surrogate homeland since they first started fleeing Cuba in the 1960s. Don't expect much in the way of sights in this district – your time here is most profitably spent out in the streets, soaking up the atmosphere. The heart of the area is Southwest 8th Street, better known by its Spanish name, Calle Ocho. Its liveliest stretch, between SW 11th and SW 17th avenues, is best enjoyed on foot, but other points of interest are more easily reached by car.

Eternal flame

Mural on Calle Ocho

🕐 You will have a much easier time in this district if you can speak a good bit of Spanish, especially in shops or when phoning establishments.

🍽 The Versailles (no. 6) is an unmissable part of the Little Havana experience. The neophyte's sampler of Cuban food includes croquettes, roast pork, and sweet plantains.

Map J–M 2–3 • El Crédito 1100 SW 8th St, at SW 11th Ave, 305-858-4162, open 8am–5:30pm Mon-Fri, 9am–4pm Sat • Versailles Restaurant, 3555 SW 8th St, at SW 35th Ave, 305-444-0240 • $$

Top 10 Attractions

1. El Crédito
2. The Brigade 2506 Memorial on Cuban Memorial Blvd
3. Domino Park
4. Plaza de la Cubanidad
5. Little Havana To Go
6. Versailles Restaurant
7. Botánica El Aguila Vidente
8. Calle Ocho Walk of Fame
9. Woodlawn Cemetery
10. José Martí Riverfront Park

El Crédito
1 Authentic cigar factory *(above)* and store selling the famous La Gloria Cubana brand. The leaves are grown in the Dominican Republic, reputedly from Cuban tobacco seeds.

Domino Park
3 For decades, male Cubans have gathered at the corner of SW 15th Ave to match wits over intense games of dominoes *(right)*. The pavilion and patio were built to accommodate the players in 1976.

Botánica shop front in Little Havana

The Brigade 2506 Memorial on Cuban Memorial Boulevard
2 An eternal flame *(top)* honors the Cuban-Americans who died in the Bay of Pigs invasion of Cuba in 1961. Other memorials pay tribute to Cuban heroes Antonio Maceo and José Martí, who fought against Spanish colonialism in the 1800s.

For more Latino arts venues, shops, and restaurants **See pp87–9**

Plaza de la Cubanidad

At the Plaza is a bronze map of Cuba and a flourish of banners *(above)* for the headquarters of Alpha 66, Miami's most hard-line anti-Castro group.

Little Havana To Go

If you're interested in Cuban memorabilia, this is the store for you. You'll find cigars, music, clothes, art, and posters for sale. There's even a replica of a 1958 telephone book, complete with names, numbers, and yellow pages.

Versailles Restaurant

A trip to Miami is incomplete without at least a snack at this legendary institution. It's a Cuban version of a fancy diner, with mirrors everywhere and a constant hubbub.

Botánica El Aguila Vidente

Santería is a Cuban religion, combining Catholicism, the Yoruba culture of Nigeria, and Native American practices. This *botánica* is one of several establishments offering paraphernalia and spiritual consultations.

Calle Ocho Walk of Fame

One of the few real sights that Little Havana has to offer the casual tourist. Imitating Hollywood, pink marble stars embedded in the sidewalks *(above)* recognize not only Cuban celebrities, beginning with salsa singer Celia Cruz in 1987, but also all famous Hispanics with any ties to South Florida.

Woodlawn Cemetery

Here lie the remains of two former Cuban presidents, dictator Gerardo Machado, as well as Nicaraguan dictator Anastasio Somoza. There's also the founder of the Cuban American National Foundation.

José Martí Riverfront Park

This small, pretty park, lying partly under I-95, was dedicated in 1985 to commemorate the Cuban struggle for freedom. The site became a Tent City for many of the 125,000 homeless Mariel boatlift refugees in 1980.

Top 10 Cuban Cultural Imports

1. Cigars
2. Salsa, mambo, bolero, merengue (rhythms)
3. Santería (mystical belief system)
4. Spanish language
5. Cafecito (Cuban coffee)
6. Black beans and plantains
7. Guayabera shirts
8. Gloria Estefan
9. The Buena Vista Social Club (movie)
10. Before Night Falls (movie)

🔟 Villa Vizcaya

A trumped-up pastiche it may be, but Villa Vizcaya is undeniably grand and glorious, with the authentic feel of a 16th-century Italian palace. Which is exactly what its makers, industrial magnate James Deering, designer Paul Chalfin, and architect F. Burrall Hoffman, intended when they built it in the early 1900s. Embodying a 400-year range of styles, both the genuine and ersatz have been skillfully assembled to evoke another culture, another continent, and another age.

The Villa and its formal gardens

Venetian-style building

🕐 Take the guided tour for lots of juicy gossip about Mr. Deering's posh ways, as well as various legends, superstitions and quirks about many of the furnishings.

💭 The museum café, located at the left end of the villa, is a pleasant culinary surprise.

Map L6 • 3251 South Miami Ave • 305-250-9133 • www.vizcaya museum.org
• 9:30am–4:30pm daily
• House closes at 5pm, gardens at 5:30pm
• Closed Christmas Day
• Adm $12; children 6–12 $5; 5 & under free

Top 10 Sights

1. Gardens
2. East Loggia
3. Italian Renaissance Living Room
4. Rococo Music Room
5. Breakfast Room
6. Empire Bathroom
7. Italian Renaissance Dining Room
8. French Rococo Reception Room
9. Neoclassical Entrance Hall and Library
10. Swimming Pool Grotto

2 East Loggia

This portico frames magnificent views of the sea and of the quaint breakwater known as the Barge. Carved in the shape of a large ship, it provides a perfect foreground to Key Biscayne, lying off the coast.

1 Gardens

The villa's gardens, will probably give you the greatest pleasure. The many splashing fountains of gracefully carved stone, statuary *(right)*, and cleverly laid-out formal plantings offer myriad harmonious and ever-changing vistas. The Secret Garden conceals the greatest artistry.

3 Italian Renaissance Living Room

The room includes a 2,000-year-old marble Roman tripod, a 15th-century Hispano-Moresque rug, a tapestry depicting the *Labors of Hercules*, and a Neapolitan altar screen.

For other historic sites See pp44–5

4 Rococo Music Room

All flowers and fluff, the room *(left)* is graced with an exquisite Italian harpsichord from 1619, a dulcimer, and a harp.

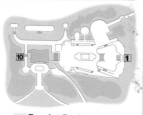

5 Breakfast Room

Four massive ceramic Chinese Foo dogs guard the steps that ascend to what is probably the most bombastic room in the house.

6 Empire Bathroom

Few bathrooms in the world are more ornate than this marble, silver, and gilded affair *(below)*. The bathtub was designed to run either fresh- or salt-water from the Bay of Biscayne.

8 French Rococo Reception Room

The assemblage is a mix of styles, but the overall look is of a salon under the 18th-century French King Louis XV. The tinted plaster ceiling is from the Rossi Palace in Venice.

7 Italian Renaissance Dining Room

Another echo of the antique Italian taste, featuring a 2,000-year-old Roman table, a pair of 16th-century tapestries, and a full set of 17th-century chairs.

Key

■ First floor
■ Second floor
■ Gardens

9 Neoclassical Entrance Hall and Library

Though still 18th-century, the mood is considerably more sober in these rooms, which are in the English Neoclassical style, inspired by the work of Robert Adam.

10 Swimming Pool Grotto

In imitation of Italian Renaissance and Baroque architects, who were in turn imitating ancient Roman styles, this pool *(above)* extends under the house and resembles a natural cave or sea grotto.

Deering's Dream

Money was no object for industrialist James Deering. He wanted his winter residence to provide a sense of family history as well as luxury. Thus he bought up bits of European pomp, shipped them over, and reassembled them on this ideal spot by the sea.

Merrick's Coral Gables Fantasies

Coral Gables, one of the country's richest neighborhoods, is a separate city within Greater Miami, and feels it. Aptly described as the City Beautiful, its swanky homes line avenues shaded by giant banyans and oak, backing up to hidden canals. Regulations ensure that new buildings use the same architectural vocabulary advocated by George Merrick when he planned the community in the 1920s. Merrick's taste sometimes ran to the Disneyesque, but undeniably he created a wonderland of a place that has not lost its aesthetic impact.

Chinese Village

George Merrick

🅾 Driving around Coral Gables can be tricky. Many of the streets have two names, and the signs are spelled out on stucco blocks at ground level, which can be hard to read, especially at night.

🅲 Sample the excellent salads and soups at Books and Books, on 265 Aragon Ave, where you can also delve deeper into local history.

Map F–G 3–4

Top 10 Sights

1 Biltmore Hotel
2 Venetian Pool
3 Chinese Village
4 Congregational Church
5 Dutch South African Village
6 French Normandy Village
7 French Country Village
8 French City Village
9 Italian Village
10 Florida Pioneer Village

Biltmore Hotel
Merrick's masterpiece has been refurbished and burnished to its original splendor, at a cost of more than $55 million *(below)*. Built in 1926, it remains one of the most stunning hotels in the country. It served as a military hospital during World War II and was a veteran's hospital until 1968. The 315-ft (96-m) near-replica of Seville's Giralda Tower is a Coral Gables landmark *(see also the Freedom Tower, p83)*.

Venetian Pool
The boast that this is the most beautiful swimming pool in the world is a fair one *(above & p99)*. Incorporating waterfalls and a cave, it was fashioned from a coral rock quarry in 1923 by Merrick's associates, Denman Fink and Phineas Paist.

Chinese Village
An entire block has been transformed into a walled Chinese enclave. The curved, glazed-tile roofs peek above the trees in vibrant colors, with Chinese red and yellow and bamboo motifs predominating.

For more on Coral Gables and the neighboring Coconut Grove district **See pp98–105**

4 Congregational Church

Coral Gables' first church *(above)*, built by Merrick in the Spanish Baroque style, is actually a replica of a church in Costa Rica.

5 Dutch South African Village

Northern Baroque frivolity meets hot-weather practicality. This charming collection of homes embodies the high-peaked façades and scrolls of typical Dutch architecture, along with the white stucco walls and red roofs associated with the Mediterranean. The style evolved as Boers adapted to African climes.

6 French Normandy Village

The most homogeneous of all the Villages at Coral Gables, this is all open timberwork, white stucco, and shake (cedar) roofs. Little alcoves and gardens here and there complete the picture-postcard look.

7 French Country Village

Seven mansions are built in various styles typical of the French country-side. Some have open timber, stone, red brick, and shake (cedar) roofs, others resemble the classic grange. One sports a marvelous turret.

8 French City Village

Here you'll find a series of nine graceful *petits palais* in the grand French style, looking almost as if a city block of Paris has been airlifted over. The most elaborate confection is on the north corner of Cellini and Hardee.

9 Italian Village

The typical country type of Italian villa, with its red tile roof and painted stucco walls. Many later constructions have carried on the theme, so the original Merrick creations are almost lost in the mix.

10 Florida Pioneer Village

Imitations of the early plantation and colonial homes built by Florida's first aristocrats. The style incorporates Neoclassical, columned porches with the stucco walls of tropical tradition.

Merrick the Visionary

Merrick's dream was to build an American Venice. The massive project spawned the biggest real estate venture of the 1920s, costing around $100 million. The hurricane of 1926 then the Wall Street crash of 1929 left Merrick's city incomplete and him destitute, but what remains of his vision is an enduring testament to his imagination.

Want to tour the Biltmore or even stay there? **See pp99 & 146**

TOP 10 Lowe Art Museum

Founded in 1950, the Lowe was built in 1950–52 thanks to a donation from philanthropists Joe and Emily Lowe, and it has since become Miami's premier art museum. More than 13,000 pieces showcase many of the world's most important artistic traditions. Collectors keep on donating works so that even more expansion to the galleries is now necessary to display them all. Nevertheless, the most significant works are always on display, unless on loan to other museums.

Museum exterior

🛒 Check the museum store for a wide array of beautifully illustrated books on the Lowe collection.

🍴 A local favorite, the Titanic Brewing Company (5813 Ponce de Leon Blvd, 305-667-2537) serves up seafood, live music, and six kinds of hand-crafted ale.

Map F3
• 1301 Stanford Drive
• 305-284-3535 • www. lowemuseum.org
• 10am–5pm Tue, Wed, Fri, Sat; noon–7pm Thu; noon–5pm Sun
• Closed Mon and national holidays
• Adm $7; concessions (students and seniors) $5; children under 12 free

Top 10 Collections

1. Egyptian
2. Greco-Roman
3. Asian
4. Ancient American
5. Native American
6. Renaissance
7. Baroque
8. Latin-American
9. African
10. 17th–Century to Contemporary European & American

Greco-Roman
2 Classical sculpture is represented by several marble carvings, including a Roman portrait bust of a matron. One of the best objects is a 6th-century BC black-figure krater *(above)*, depicting Apollo, Artemis, and Leto.

Egyptian
1 The Egyptian collection is tiny but fascinating, especially the Coptic textiles, several intriguing fragments of which are displayed in frames on the wall. There is also a jewel-like portrait sarcophagus mask, intended to resemble the features of the deceased.

Asian
3 One of the Museum's strongest collections, featuring magnificent Chinese Neolithic ceramics *(left)*, as well as bronze and jade pieces and other ceramics from Neolithic times to the 20th century. There is also a strong representation of classic, folk and tribal art from India.

For more fabulous museums in Miami and the Keys
See pp42–3

4 Ancient American

An excellent collection covers all eras and areas, from about 1500 BC to the 16th century. A Mayan pot with a jaguar and human bone design is very forceful. The silver disk from 14th-century Peru *(below)* is a very rare piece.

5 Native American

A Seminole shoulder bag *(left)* is the pride of this collection, beautifully executed using thousands of tiny, colored-glass trade beads. The Najavo, Apache, and Hopi art forms include textiles, pottery, basketry, and *kachina* dolls.

6 Renaissance

The small but exquisite collection of mostly Italian paintings includes works by Tintoretto, Dosso Dossi, Palma Vecchio, Bicci di Lorenzo, and Cozzarelli *(right)*. There are also two lovely terra-cottas by Andrea della Robbia.

7 Baroque

This period in European art is epitomized here by painters from many countries, such as Jacob Jordaens, Lucas Cranach the Elder, Jusepe de Ribera, and Francesco Guardi.

8 Latin-American

Important holdings of 20th-century art by Hispanic artists include Fernando Botero of Colombia and Carlos Alfonzo, who was born in Cuba.

9 African

Works as diverse as the 16th-century cast bronze ring of the Yoruba people, depicting ritual decapitation, a Nok terra-cotta figure *(right)*, and an Elpe or Ngbe society emblem assemblage all have an undeniable potency.

10 17th-Century to Contemporary European & American

Some extraordinary works on permanent display include *Americanoom* by Chryssa, *Modular Painting in Four Panels* by Roy Lichtenstein, *Le Neveu de Rameau* by Frank Stella, *Football Player (left)* by Duane Hanson, and *Rex* by Deborah Butterfield.

Museum Guide

The Lowe is located in the middle of the campus of the University of Miami, which is in southern Coral Gables and is easily accessible by the Miami Metrorail – just follow the signs. There is no particular order in which you are expected to visit the collections. Remember that several of the galleries are always given over to special temporary exhibitions.

⑩ The Wolfsonian

Strangely, the museum began life in the 1920s as the Washington Storage Company – Miami's wealthier winter residents used to store their valuables here when they were away. Eventually, in 1984, one Mitchell Wolfson, Jr. decided to buy it outright as a home for his vast assemblage of the rich detritus of modernity. It opened to the public in 1995. Over 70,000 objects include decorative and propaganda art, furniture, and much, much more.

Façade of Mediterranean-Revival Building

🔎 Ask about the tour that is available upon request and check the museum store for its excellent catalogs.

🍴 In the Moderne mood, the popular Streamline Moderne Diner on 11th St & Washington Ave (305-534-6373) has malted milk shakes and hamburgers, as well as more sophisticated fare.

Map R4 • 1001 Washington Ave, Miami Beach • 305-531-1001 • www.wolfsonian.org • noon–6pm Mon, Tue, Sat, and Sun; noon–9pm Thu and Fri • Closed national holidays • Café Dynamo open daily • Adults $5; seniors and students $3

Top 10 Exhibits

1. Bridge Tender's House
2. Mediterranean-Revival Building
3. Entrance Hall
4. Fountain
5. The Wrestler
6. Art Deco Mail Box
7. Ceiling, Chandeliers, and Brackets
8. Wooden Staircase
9. Clarke Window
10. Temporary Exhibits

1 Bridge Tender's House

Standing just to the north of the Wolfsonian's entrance, this remarkable 1939 building is a stainless-steel hexagonal structure designed in the Art Moderne style.

2 Mediterranean-Revival Building

The Spanish Baroque-style relief around the main entrance is a striking feature. The bronze flagpole brackets and finials date from 1914.

The Wrestler

3 Entrance Hall

The massive ceiling supports *(below)* reflect the Mediterranean-Revival style of the façade and are original to the building. So are the terra-cotta floors, the woodwork over the doors leading to the elevator vestibule, and the rough stucco walls. The stonework is unfinished according to Mediterranean-Revival tenets

Fountain
4 Set under a skylight, the fountain was fashioned from an elaborate Deco window grille taken from the Norris Theater in Pennsylvania. Composed of over 200 gilded and glazed terra-cotta tiles, the richly floral decorative scheme belies the careful geometrical structure of the piece.

The Wrestler
5 The symbol of the Wolfsonian *(left)* confronts visitors as they approach the elevator. Its brawny, nude, life-sized form is made entirely of aluminum, perhaps the quintessential metal of 20th-century modernity.

Wooden Staircase
8 This fine piece of modern woodcraft *(right)* is fashioned from pine and steel. It came from the Curtis Bok residence, Gulph Mills, Pennsylvania, designed by Wharton Esherick in 1935.

Clarke Window
9 The stained-glass window *(below)* made for the League of Nations' International Labor Building in Geneva, Switzerland, in 1926–30, is an impressive piece.

Key
- First floor
- Fifth floor
- Sixth floor
- Seventh floor

Miami's Top 10

Art Deco Mailbox
6 To the left of the elevator is a wonderful 1929 Art Deco bronze mailbox *(left)*, originally in New York Central Railroad Terminal, Buffalo.

Ceiling, Chandeliers, and Brackets
7 These unique decorative features come from a 1920s Miami car showroom and a restaurant in Missouri.

Temporary Exhibits
10 Much of the available gallery space is used throughout the year for special exhibits, often with compelling themes that reflect the subjects of research at the University. Propaganda art has featured, showing how savvy designers have called upon the science of psychology to create highly persuasive images for businesses and governments.

Orientation
The Wolfsonian is both a museum and a design research institute attached to Florida International University. Three of the floors are used for offices, storage, and a library, and are not normally open to the public. Your tour should begin outside, progress to the Entrance Hall, then up the back elevator to floors 5, 6, and 7.

Gold Coast Highway A1A

The very best way to get a feel for the quality of life along the Gold Coast is to take a leisurely drive north on A1A. The road hugs the beach almost all the way and passes through some of the most beautiful natural settings and some of the wealthiest communities in the U.S. The 50-mile (80-km) route can be traversed in a day, but it's worth spending more time to take in the local color, from tropical nature preserves to fabulous mansions, all within sight of the sugary blond sands and the azure Atlantic.

John U. Lloyd Park

The Broadwalk

🌀 To get the most out of Fort Lauderdale, take the three-hour Jungle Queen Cruise (954-462-5596).

🍽 Lunch in Fort Lauderdale at Noodles Panini, 821 East Las Olas Blvd (954-462-1514). At dinnertime, head for Las Olas Café, 922 East Las Olas Blvd (954-524-4300) or Bistro Mezzaluna, 741 SE 17th St Causeway, (954-522-6620).

• Map D3, IGFA Fishing Hall of Fame and Museum, 300 Gulf Stream Way, Dania Beach (954-927-2628)
• Map D2, Flagler Museum, 1 Whitehall Way, Palm Beach (561-655-2833) • Norton Museum of Art, 1451 S. Olive Ave, West Palm Beach (561-832-5196)

Top 10 Sights
1. The Broadwalk
2. John U. Lloyd Beach State Park
3. South Florida Museum of Natural History
4. Las Olas Boulevard, Fort Lauderdale
5. Bonnet House
6. Gumbo Limbo Nature Center
7. Worth Avenue, Palm Beach
8. Flagler Museum
9. The Breakers
10. Norton Museum of Art

1 The Broadwalk
This famous stretch of Hollywood Beach *(above)* runs from South Sunset Road to Sheridan, where 2.5 miles (4 km) of shops, bars, and restaurants abound, best of all the French-Caribbean fusion of Sugar Reef.

Flagler Museum

2 John U. Lloyd Beach State Park
This long barrier island of gardens and forests commands views of busy Port Everglades and a beach historically significant as one designated for African-Americans, in the days of segregation. It's now a gay destination *(see p52)*.

3 IGFA Fishing Hall of Fame and Museum
This facility appeals to all ages and has seven different galleries highlighting the creatures of the sea, a fun discovery room for children, a virtual fishing exhibit (where you can hold a fishing pole and feel the pull of the fish), and a vast wetland area.

Fort Lauderdale has many facilities for gay visitors
See pp52–3 & 153

4 Las Olas Boulevard, Fort Lauderdale

Fort Lauderdale's main street *(above)* boasts upscale shops and excellent eateries. At the river end, Las Olas Riverfront is a colorful theme mall, from which the Riverfront Canal Cruise departs *(see panel)*.

5 Bonnet House

This period home (built 1920) is full of the personality of the couple who created it, Frederic and Evelyn Bartlett. They were both artists, as is evident from the highly original murals, and the somewhat eccentric tropical gardens.

6 Gumbo Limbo Nature Center

An informative center, with a boardwalk that winds through mangroves and hammocks (raised areas) in Red Reef Park. It takes its name from the gumbo limbo tree, which has distinctive, red peeling bark.

7 Worth Avenue, Palm Beach

The street *(above)* for local and visiting VIPs to select this week's wardrobe and perhaps a little objet d'art.

9 The Breakers

The third hotel to be built on this site, the first two having burned down. However, the aura of America's Gilded Age (1880–1910) still clings to every aspect of this stylish abode *(below)*, from the frescoed Italianate ceilings to the countless crystal chandeliers.

8 Flagler Museum

The "Taj Mahal of America," was Henry M. Flagler's *(see p45)* wedding gift to his third wife, who was half his age and an heiress herself. The trappings of royalty are everywhere, down to the hand-painted dinner service that once belonged to a French king.

10 Norton Museum of Art

Perhaps Florida's finest museum of art, featuring Impressionists, Modern Americans, and much more *(see p42)*.

All That Glitters

Here, all that glitters probably is gold! The Gold Coast may have got its name from gold doubloons that Spanish galleons used to carry along the intracoastal waterways, but these days the term refers more to the golden lifestyle of the many millionaires and billionaires who have winter homes here.

Want to continue farther north on A1A? **See p128**

TOP 10 Key West

First recorded by Spanish explorers in 1513, this tiny island (key), just two miles by four (3.2 x 6.4 km), has changed in status from a pirates' den to the most prosperous city per capita in the US. Always attracting free-thinkers, eccentrics, and misfits, Key West has a uniquely oddball character that is still apparent despite the upscale tourism that has developed since the 1990s. The self-named Conch ("conk") inhabitants include many gays, writers, artists, and New-Agers.

Shipwreck Museum

Sunset, Mallory Square

You can travel by road from the mainland all the way through the Keys, crossing various bridges, to Key West.

The Conch Tour Train, boarding at Mallory Square, provides an overview of Old Town.

Rick's Blue Heaven, at 729 Thomas St, is the quintessence of old Key West: a Caribbean menu and a garden with trademark Key West chickens and cats wandering around. (*Also see p125 for the best of Conch dining.*)

Map A6 • Key West Information Center, 1601 N. Roosevelt Blvd 1-888-222-5148 • www.Keywestinfo.com • Museums 9am–5pm (approx.) daily; adm • Cemetery sunrise–6pm daily; free • Fort Zachary, Taylor 8am–sunset daily; adm

Top 10 Sights

1. Duval Street
2. Mallory Square
3. Bahama Village
4. Mel Fisher's Maritime Heritage Society Museum
5. Hemingway House
6. Audubon House and Tropical Gardens
7. Key West Cemetery
8. Key West Art and History Museum
9. Lighthouse Museum
10. Fort Zachary Taylor Historic State Park

Duval Street

1 Duval Street
Running from the Gulf of Mexico at the north end to the Atlantic Ocean in the south, the main street of Old Town is the place to do the "Duval Crawl." This is the arduous task of strolling the street and stopping in at all of the 100 or so bars, pubs, and clubs that line Duval and its neighboring roads.

2 Mallory Square
Every evening at sunset, the fun-loving citizens of the self-styled "Conch Republic" throw a party in this large, seaside square, complete with entertainers of all sorts.

3 Bahama Village
An archway across Petronia Street at Duval announces that you are entering this largely African-American neighborhood,

which offers a tiny slice of Island culture (*left*). A block in is the Bahama Market, featuring handicrafts; farther along is Rick's Blue Heaven (*see panel*).

For more on Key West's local architectural style **See p47**

4 Mel Fisher's Maritime Heritage Society Museum
Dedicated to the lure and lore of sunken treasure and the equipment *(left)* that has been used to retrieve it. Most impressive are the gold artifacts from 17th-century Spanish galleons.

Hemingway House 5
"Papa" Ernest Hemingway lived in this Spanish colonial-style house built of coral rock from 1931–40, and wrote many of his works here. Remnants of his stay include boxing gloves *(right)* and supposed descendants of his six-toed cats.

6 Audubon House and Tropical Gardens
A glimpse into mid-19th-century life on the island. The audio tour is excellent, as "ghosts" of the family who lived here take you through the rooms.

7 Key West Cemetery
The tombs are raised to avoid flooding and because the soil is mostly hard coral rock. Famously droll epitaphs include "I told you I was sick" on the tomb of a notorious hypochondriac.

9 Lighthouse Museum
Built in 1848, Key West's lighthouse was capable of beaming light 25 miles (40 km) out to sea. Climb the 88 steps to enjoy panoramic seascapes and views of the town.

8 Key West Art and History Museum
Housed in the imposing old Customs House are paintings of some of the island's eccentrics and notables, along with accounts of life here in various epochs.

10 Fort Zachary Taylor Historic State Park
The 1866 brick fort is now a military museum *(left)* with a fine collection of Civil War artifacts. The island's best beach is nearby.

Top 10 Denizens

1	**Henry Flagler** Standard Oil magnate
2	**José Martí** Cuban freedom fighter
3	**John James Audubon** Naturalist
4	**Ernest Hemingway** Writer
5	**Harry S. Truman** President
6	**Tennessee Williams** Playwright
7	**Robert Frost** Poet
8	**John Dewey** Educator-philosopher
9	**Jimmy Buffett** Singer-songwriter
10	**Tallulah Bankhead** Actress

For a day's itinerary, shops, restaurants, and regular events in Key West **See pp117–25**

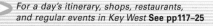

The Everglades

One of the planet's most fascinating ecosystems, the Everglades is a vast, shallow river system of swamps and wetlands, whose waters can take a year or more to meander from the Kissimmee River, northwest of Miami, into Florida Bay. At least 45 plant varieties grow here that are found nowhere else on Earth. It is also home to over 350 kinds of bird, 500 types of fish, and dozens of reptile and mammal species.

Alligator, Billie Swamp Wildlife Park

Pinelands in the heart of the Everglades

🕐 Try to visit the Everglades early in the morning, when many animals are active. Protect yourself from biting insects, sun, and heat, and keep to the boardwalks.

🍴 The Swamp Water Café on the Big Cypress Reservation (863-983-6101) offers alligator tail nuggets, catfish filets, and frog legs, alongside the usual hamburgers, etc, all at reasonable prices.

Maps B–C 3–5 • Everglades National Park 305-242-7700 • Gulf Coast Visitor Center, Everglades City (239) 695-3311 • Big Cypress Swamp: Oasis Visitor Center (239) 695-1201 • Shark Valley Information Center 305-221-8776 • Flamingo Visitor Center (239) 695-2945 • Fakahatchee Strand (239) 695-4593 • Corkscrew Swamp, 375 Sanctuary Rd (239) 348-9151

Top 10 Sights

1. Tamiami Trail (US 41)
2. Everglades National Park
3. Big Cypress Swamp
4. Shark Valley
5. Ah-Tah-Thi-Ki and Billie Swamp
6. Anhinga and Gumbo Limbo Trails
7. Mahogany Hammock
8. Flamingo
9. Fakahatchee Strand
10. Corkscrew Swamp

1 Tamiami Trail (US 41)

This was the first road to open up the area by linking the Atlantic and Gulf coasts. It passes pioneer camps, such as Everglades City and Chokoloskee, which have barely changed since the late 1800s. They mark the western entrance to Everglades National Park.

2 Everglades National Park

The park covers about one-fifth of the Everglades. There are elevated boardwalks, tours, canoe rental, camping and hotel and *chikee* lodgings (Seminole-style huts).

3 Big Cypress Swamp

This vast, shallow wetland basin is not a true swamp but a range of wet and dry habitats determined by slight differences in elevation. It is home to hundreds of species including the Florida panther.

4 Shark Valley

This area, only 17 miles (27 km) from the western edge of Miami, has a 15-mile (24-km) loop road that you can travel by bicycle or on a narrated tram ride. It ends at a tower *(left)* that affords great views

5 Ah-Tah-Thi-Ki and Billie Swamp

A museum here is devoted to Native American Seminole culture *(left)* – *ah-tah-thi-ki* means "a place to learn, or remember." A wildlife park nearby has exhilarating airboat rides and informative Buggy Eco-Tours, from which you might spot alligators.

6 Anhinga and Gumbo Limbo Trails

Both of these popular trails begin at the Royal Palm Visitor Center, the site of Florida's first state park.

7 Mahogany Hammock

Farther along toward Flamingo, you'll come to one of the park's largest hammocks (fertile mounds), where a trail meanders through dense tropical growth. This is home to the largest mahogany tree in the country and colorful tree snails.

Preserving the Everglades

The Everglades evolved over a period of more than 6 million years, but humans almost destroyed its fragile balance in less than 100. In the 1920s, the Hoover Dike closed off Lake Okeechobee, the main source of Everglades water, and Highway 41 was built, further blocking its natural flow. Thankfully, environmentalist Marjory Stoneman Douglas reversed the march toward doom. Today, there are plans to build levees around the Everglades, to help keep the vital moisture in.

9 Fakahatchee Strand

One of Florida's wildest areas, a 20-mile (32-km) slough (muddy backwater), noted for the largest stand of native royal palms in the US, unique air plants, and rare orchids. There are boardwalks *(right)* and rangers on hand.

10 Corkscrew Swamp

A boardwalk takes you through various habitats, including a stand of old cypress full of nesting birds. The endangered wood stork has been spotted here.

8 Flamingo

Flamingo is called home by only a handful of park rangers these days, but it was once an outpost for hunters, fishermen, and smugglers, accessible only by water. Sportfishing, canoeing, bird-watching, and hiking are very good here.

 For routes through the Everglades and places to eat
See pp127 & 130

Left **South Pointe Beach** Center **Matheson Hammock Beach** Right **Key West**

TOP 10 Beaches

1 Lummus Park Beach

This broad, long, and well-maintained stretch of sand is, for many, the epitome of South Beach. In season, bronzed bodies line up row after row, some with boom boxes blasting, others just catching the rays. The more active play volleyball, do gymnastics, and, of course, take to the waves. From 5th to 11th Streets, women can go topless. ◈ *Map S3*

2 Haulover Park Beach

Haulover has been spared the sight of high-rise development. The dune-backed beach lies along the eastern side of the park, and to the north it has become the only nude beach in the county, part of it gay. ◈ *Map H2 • Just north of Bal Harbour*

3 South Pointe Park Beach

Though not well known for its beaches, the park's northern part is popular with surfers, and you can watch cruise ships gliding in and out of the Port of Miami.

It's also great for walks, and there's a fitness course, an observation tower, charcoal grills, picnic spots, and playgrounds. ◈ *Map S6*

4 Sunny Isles Beach

More noteworthy for its 1950s' tourist-resort kitsch than for its rocky sand, this strip is popular with older tourists, as well as surfers and sailors. Souvenir shops and hotels indulge in campy architectural fancies, featuring exotic themes along Collins (A1A) between 160th & 185th Streets. ◈ *Map H1*

5 Hobie Island Beach and Virginia Key Beach

While Hobie is popular with windsurfers, Virginia Key – neighbor to Key Biscayne and similarly shrouded in Australian pines – has no residents and few visitors. Under Old South segregation, it was the only Miami beach African-Americans were allowed to use. Once you walk through the vegetation, the

Haulover Park Beach

 South Beach, Miami's best-known stretch, is covered on **pp8–9**

Typical beach in Miami

2-mile (3-km) beach here is fine and relatively empty. Both are excellent for children due to the warm bay waters, but Virginia Key has deep waters and possible undertow. ◈ *Map H3*

6 Crandon Beach
One of several South Florida beaches that are rated among the top ten in the entire US, this one is on upper Key Biscayne *(see p72)*. ◈ *Map H3–4*

7 Bill Baggs Cape Florida State Park
Also rated as one of the top ten beaches in the US, located at the pristine southern tip of Key Biscayne *(see pp72–3)*. ◈ *Map H4*

8 Matheson Hammock Park Beach
Considerably battered by 1992's Hurricane Andrew, this 100-acre (40-ha) park is making a comeback. Developed in the 1930s by Commodore J. W. Matheson, it features the man-made Atoll Pool, a salt-water swimming pool encircled by sand and palm trees right alongside Biscayne Bay. The tranquil beach is popular with families and enjoys warm, safe waters surrounded by tropical hardwood forests. Other attractions include walking trails through the mangrove swamp. ◈ *Map G4 • N of Fairchild Tropical Garden*

9 Bahia Honda State Park
Frequently voted the best beach in the US, Bahia Honda is noted for its perfect sands, great watersports, and exotic tropical forests *(see p117)*. ◈ *Map B6*

10 Key West Beaches
Key West's relatively modest beaches are lined up along the southern side of the island, stretching from Fort Zachary Taylor State Park in the west to Smathers Beach in the east. The latter is the largest and most popular, but locals favor the former because it's less crowded. For convenience, the beach at the bottom of Duval Street, at the Southernmost Point in the US, is fine, friendly, and full of refreshment options. ◈ *Map A6*

Left **Swimming with turtles** Center **Fort Lauderdale beach** Right **Scuba diving shop**

🔟 Snorkeling and Diving

1 John Pennekamp Coral Reef State Park

Many say this park offers some of the best snorkeling in the world. Various boats can also be rented here, or you can take a more leisurely view from a glass-bottomed boat *(see p115)*.

2 Biscayne National Underwater Park

Closer to Miami than John Pennekamp, the Biscayne National Underwater Park has almost as many good snorkeling possibilities. Here you'll find vivid coral reefs to dive among, and mangrove swamps to explore by canoe *(see p108)*.

Looe Key sign

3 Looe Key National Marine Sanctuary

A brilliant coral dive location, and the closest great snorkeling to Key West. Accessible from Bahia Honda State Park *(see p117)*.

Queen angelfish

4 Dry Tortugas National Park

Located almost 70 miles (110 km) west of Key West, these seven islands and their surrounding waters comprise a fantastic park. The snorkeling sights are exceptional, due to the shallow waters and abundance of marine life. You can snorkel directly off the beaches of Fort Jefferson or take one of the trips to the wreck of the *Windjammer*, which sank on Loggerhead Reef in 1907. Tropical fish, lobster, and even goliath grouper can be found *(see p129)*.

5 Key Biscayne Parks

Both Crandon and Bill Baggs Parks have excellent areas for snorkeling, in some of Miami's cleanest, clearest waters *(see pp72–3)*.

6 Fort Lauderdale Waters

Fort Lauderdale has been awarded the Blue Wave Beaches certification for spotless sands and crystal waters, which add up to superior underwater viewing. Many of the most interesting parts of the three-tiered natural reef system here are close to the shore, though most require a short boat ride. In addition, more than 80 artificial reefs have been built to enhance the growth of marine flora and fauna. Ocean Promotion is one of the

Be safe in the waters – See p139

Diving off the Florida Keys

companies organizing snorkeling and scuba trips. 🕉 *Map D3 • Ocean promotion 954-561-4499, www.florida-adventure.com/ocean promotion*

7 Red Reef Park

Boca Raton is famous for its extensive and beautifully maintained parks, and its Red Reef Park offers some of the best beaches and snorkeling in the area. An artificial reef, clearly marked on the park's visitor map, can provide hours of delightful undersea viewing and is suitable for youngsters. The Gumbo Limbo Nature Center is just across the street. 🕉 *Map D3 • 1801 North Ocean Blvd, Boca Raton • 9am–noon Mon–Sat, noon–4pm Sun • 561-338-1473 • www.gumbolimbo.org*

8 Palm Beach

The Breakers and Four Seasons hotels *(see p146)* both offer snorkeling options along the Palm Beach coast. 🕉 *Map D2*

9 Bahia Honda State Park Waters

The beautiful, sandy beach of Bahia Honda in the Keys – often lauded as one of the best beaches in the US – has good waters for swimming and snorkeling. Equipment rentals are available *(see p117)*.

10 Key West Waters

Take the plunge right off the beach at Fort Zachary Taylor State Park, or join an expedition out to the reefs that lie all around this island *(see pp26–7)*. There are plenty of trips offered by local companies, most of them taking three to four hours in total, including at least an hour and a half of reef time. They usually leave twice a day, at around 9am and again at about 1pm. 🕉 *Map A6*

Beach at Key West

Left **In-line skating** Center **Cycling** Right **Tennis**

TOP 10 Sports Activities

Beach volleyball

1 Volleyball
On every beach in South Florida, you'll find nets and likely team members ready to go. This is the quintessential beach sport, where taking a tumble in the sand is part of the fun!

2 In-line Skating
Gliding along on little wheels is probably the number one activity for the terminally tanned of South Florida. Down on flaunt-it-all South Beach, you can rent in-line skates or get fitted for your very own pair.

3 Windsurfing and Surfing
Miami has good prevailing winds and both calm and surging waters: so, plenty of scope for good surfing. The Keys tend to be good for windsurfing only, as the surrounding reefs break the big waves.

Surfing

4 Jet-Skiing and Parasailing
Not as challenging as they may appear and, of course, great fun! In Miami, the placid intracoastal waterways are best, but it's the Keys that have the most superlative conditions, especially Key West. 🕸 *Sunset Waterports 305-296-2554 • Sebago Watersports 305-292-2411 • Island Water Sports 305-296-1754 • Key Cat 305-240-1075*

5 Boating and Kayaking
Striking out on your own in a kayak, you can explore the colorful waters around the Keys, or slip into the winding mangrove creeks off Florida Bay. While at the other end of the scale, you could climb aboard historic schooners the *Western Union* or the *America*. 🕸 *Kayaking 305-296-3212 or 305-295-9898 • Schooner trips 305-292-1766 or 305-292-7787*

6 Dolphin Swims
These unforgettable experiences are available at Miami's Seaquarium and all along the Keys *(see pp115–16)*. Be sure to make reservations as much as a month in advance. Otherwise, try a Dolphin Watch. 🕸 *Sunny Days Catamarans 305-293-5144*

The top sports activities on Miami Beach and Key Biscayne are listed on **p74**

Boating

7 Bicycling

An excellent way to explore South Beach, Key Biscayne, or Key West. Rental shops abound, and there are a good number of excellent bike trails in the Everglades, too.

8 Fishing

There are any number of companies that will take you deep-sea fishing, while freshwater fishing is good at Amelia Earhart Park or Lake Okeechobee. ✆ *Reward Fleet, at the Miami Beach Marina, 305-372-9470 (www.fishingmiami.com)* • *In Key West 305-304-2483 or 305-304-8888* • *In Fort Lauderdale (954) 527-3460*

Fishing from Miami Beach Marina

9 Golf

No end of opportunities throughout South Florida. Many resorts have their own courses; one of the best in Greater Miami is the Jacaranda Golf Club in Plantation, voted South Florida's Golf Club of the Year. ✆ *Jacaranda Golf Club 954-472-5836 or 1-888-955-1234* • *Sunrise Country Club (954) 742-4333*

10 Tennis

South Floridians love this game, and there are public and private courts everywhere. Key Biscayne is the top choice, of course, where the Nasdaq 100 Open is held every March *(see sidebar)*.

Spectator Sports

1 Football

Miami's contender in the National Football League is the Miami Dolphins. ✆ *Pro Player Stadium , 2269 NW 199th St*

2 Jai Alai

This is often called the world's fastest game. ✆ *Miami Fronton, 3500 NW 37th Ave*

3 Horse Racing

Two of the best places are Gulfstream Park, and Calder Racecourse. ✆ *Gulfstream Park, 901 S Federal Hwy, Hallandale* • *open Jan–Apr* ✆ *Calder Racecourse 21001 NW 27th Ave* • *May–Dec*

4 Dog Racing

While running greyhound races part of the year, Flagler has year-round simulcasting of dog and horse races. ✆ *Flagler Dog Track, 401 NW 37th Ave at NW 7th St*

5 Stock-Car Racing

Homestead Miami Speedway hosts several big events every year. ✆ *1 Speedway Blvd*

6 Tennis

The Nasdaq-100 Open is one of the world's biggest non-Grand Slam tournaments. ✆ *Crandon Park, Key Biscayne*

7 Polo

This is well represented in posh Palm Beach County. ✆ *3667 120th Ave S, Wellington*

8 Basketball

The Miami Heat calls the American Airlines Arena home. ✆ *601 Biscayne Blvd*

9 Ice Hockey

The Florida Panthers play out by the Everglades at BankAtlantic Center. ✆ *1 Panther Parkway, Sunrise*

10 Baseball

Twice world champions Florida Marlins play at Pro Player Stadium ✆ *2269 NW 199th St*

➤ The top sports activities in the Keys are listed on **p120**

 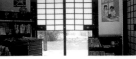

Left **Lion Country Safari** Right **Morikami Museum**

Parks, Gardens, and Zoos

1 Fairchild Tropical Garden

One of the best of South Florida's ravishing tropical gardens *(see p107)*.

2 Parrot Jungle Island

A thoroughly enjoyable place, recently relocated to Biscayne Bay, with a petting farm for children to get close to the animals *(see p71)*.

Miami Metrozoo

3 Miami Metrozoo

An extremely well-conceived and beautifully maintained animal park, divided into habitats that imitate Australasia, Asia, and Africa. It takes at least three hours to walk around it all (the time is well worth spending), or take the 45-minute tram tour or Zoofari monorail, the price of which is included in the entrance fee *(see p107)*.

4 Monkey Jungle

Here you have the chance to walk through the apes' own jungle – where you're the one in the cage! *(See p107.)*

5 Lion Country Safari

Besides effective recreations of habitats in Kenya, Zimbabwe, Mozambique, the Kalihari, and the Serengeti, the extensive park also features evocations of an Indian forest and the Great Plains of North America. Drive or take a guided bus tour through over 500 acres (200 ha) of wildlife. ◈ *2003 Lion Country Safari Road, Loxahatchee • Map C2–D3 • 561-793-1084 • www.lioncountrysafari.com • Adm*

6 Fruit & Spice Park

The only tropical botanical garden of its kind in the United States. The plants are grouped

Fairchild Tropical Garden

 Many of Miami's luxury and resort hotels have stunning tropical gardens – See pp146 & 148

by country of origin, and the tropical climate here sustains over 100 varieties of citrus plant, 65 of banana, and 40 of grape. The park also houses the largest bamboo collection in the US. In the store you'll find imported fruit products, including dried and canned fruit, juices, jams, teas, and unusual seeds (see p109).

7 Red Reef Park
This wonderful park in Boca Raton contains the Gumbo Limbo Center, which offers nature walks over a coastal hammock (raised area). There is also an artificial reef (see p33).

8 Morikami Museum and Japanese Gardens
Blossoming from a Japanese colony founded here in 1905, the Yamato-kan villa is surrounded by formal Japanese gardens of various ages: a Heian (9th- to 12th-century) shinden-style garden, a paradise garden emulating those of the 13th–14th centuries, rock gardens, a flat garden, and a modern romantic garden. Serenity and restraint amid the tropical effusiveness of South Florida. ◈ 4000 Morikami Park Road, Delray Beach • Map D3 • 561-495-0233 • www.morikami.org • Adm

9 Flamingo Gardens
These beautiful gardens began life in 1927 as a weekend retreat for the citrus-farming Wray family. The lush botanical gardens and bird sanctuary are worth at least half a day. There's a "free-flight" aviary, featuring a mass of Florida birds, including the comical roseate spoonbill and, of course, the flamingo. The rare bald eagle has also made a home here. ◈ 3750 South Flamingo Rd, Davie/Fort Lauderdale • Map D3 • 954-473-2955 • www.flamingogardens.org • Adm

Flamingo Gardens

10 Nancy's Secret Garden
Lose yourself, or perhaps find yourself, in this impossibly lush acre of land just a block off Duval Street. Intensely beautiful, the garden emanates a palpable sense of peace and contentment. The ravishing varieties of flora – orchids, bromeliads, rare palms – and the well-loved parrots put any visitor at ease. ◈ 1 Free-School Lane, off Simonton, between Fleming and Southard • 305-294-0015 • Adm

Left **Performance at the Colony** Center **Lincoln Theater** Right **Florida Grand Opera**

🔟 Lively Arts

1 Colony Theater

Starting out as an Art Deco movie theater in 1934, the Colony is now a state-of-the-art venue for some of the city's best classical music concerts, dance, theatrical performances, and experimental film. ◈ *1040 Lincoln Rd, at Lenox Ave, South Beach • Map Q2 • 305-674-1040*

Ballerina, Miami City Ballet

2 Miami Performing Arts Center

This spectacular new center is located in Downtown Miami. It includes three state-of-the-art theaters, an education center, a large outdoor plaza, and a restored 1929 Art Deco tower. Resident companies include Florida Grand Opera and Miami City Ballet. ◈ *1300 Biscayne Blvd • 305-949-6722 • www.miamipac.org*

3 Jackie Gleason Theater of the Performing Arts

The theater is unmistakable for its electric blue color and Lichtenstein's *Mermaid* outside.

For over 50 years it has brought the best of Broadway to South Florida. ◈ *1700 Washington Ave, South Beach • Map R2 • 305-673-7300 • www.gleasontheater.com*

4 Miracle Theater

The 1940s Deco-style movie theater was converted into a playhouse in 1995 and was soon winning accolades for musicals such as *West Side Story*. ◈ *280 Miracle Mile, Coral Gables • 305-444-9293 • www.actorsplayhouse.org*

5 Coconut Grove Playhouse

In 1956, Samuel Beckett's *Waiting for Godot* premiered at this restored 1920s venue. Nothing so history-making has since occured, but the likes of Kathleen Turner and Jimmy Buffett perform. ◈ *3500 Main Highway • 305-442-4000*

6 Miami City Ballet

This is a world-class ballet company, under the direction of Edward Villella. The repertoire

Jackie Gleason Theater of the Performing Arts

Miami City Ballet venue

consists of some 85 ballets.
⊗ *2200 Liberty Ave, Miami Beach* • *305-929-7010* • *www.miamicityballet.org*

7 Florida Grand Opera

The opera house sometimes brings global luminaries to Miami, but their programs also feature new works, such as the compelling *Balseros*, based on the trials of Cuban refugees who attempt to reach Florida by raft.
⊗ *1200 Coral Way* • *1-800-741-1010*
• *www.fgo.org*

8 Gusman Center for the Performing Arts

The major Downtown venue offers a program of plays, music, dance, and film *(see p84)*.

9 Lincoln Theater

The Lincoln is home to the New World Symphony, which is made up of music college graduates. The young virtuosos perform an incredible mix of gospel, Piazzolla tango, symphonies, and chamber works. ⊗ *555 Lincoln Rd, South Beach* • *Map R2* • *305-673-3330* • *www.nws.org*

10 Miami-Dade County Auditorium

Built in 1951, this Deco-style venue is proud to have been one of the first in the country to host Luciano Pavarotti when he was still a virtual unknown. Operas, concerts, and touring events all benefit from the excellent acoustics in the auditorium. ⊗ *2901 W Flagler St* • *305-547-5414*

Top 10 Entertainers

1 Jackie Gleason
"The Great One," who practically invented early American television, brought his *Jackie Gleason Show* permanently to Miami in 1964.

2 Don Johnson
Miami Vice-roy himself, the King of 1980s Cool helped put hip "new" South Beach on the map *(see p72)*.

3 Cher
You can see where the ageless diva and Sonny lived on the water in Fort Lauderdale and South Beach.

4 Madonna
She had a palatial spread next to Vizcaya for a while, and still owns a piece of the Delano Hotel restaurant.

5 Dave Barry
The newspaper humorist and author has helped to create Miami's image as an over-the-top urban free-for-all.

6 Gloria Estefan
For many, the symbol of unstoppable Cuban Power, this talented pop songstress has succeeded in building an impressive cultural and real-estate empire.

7 Rosie O'Donnell
The talkshow hostess calls Miami home and is involved in local politics *(see also p49)*.

8 Jennifer Lopez
This Latino actress and songstress has owned a mansion and estate at Miami Beach since 2002.

9 Ricky Martin
Another Latino superstar who owns real estate here.

10 Tito Puente, Jr.
The talented musician son of the famed Latin bandleader makes South Florida home, where he promotes gay causes.

⮕ *For the best Latino arts venues* **See p87**

Left **Coconut Grove Arts Festival** Center **Dade County Fair** Right **International Mango Festival**

Festivals

1 Key West Fantasy Fest

For two weeks leading up to Halloween, Key West gives itself over to non-stop celebration. Then, on the Saturday before the 31st, a parade, featuring lavish floats and outlandish costumes, departs from Mallory Square and slowly winds down Duval Street. In a spirit of free abandon, many revelers go nude, except for a bit of body paint here and a feather or two there. ◈ *Map A6 • Last 2 weeks in Oct*

Winter Party

2 Carnaval Miami

For the Cuban district, March is a time of dancing and singing in the streets – to Latin jazz, pop, flamenco and tango. It culminates on the second Sunday with what claims to be the largest party in the world. Twenty-three blocks of Little Havana are closed off and performers line the way, along with food stalls of ethnic favorites. An enormous fireworks display brings a resounding finale to the festivities. ◈ *8th St from 4th–27th Aves • Map K3 • Approx first ten days of Mar*

3 Winter Party and White Party

These annual gay beach parties are principally about buff young wannabes chasing international-circuit models. Still, one appreciative participant praised the events as "a sea of beautiful, naked men." Well, not entirely naked, but nearly so. Pumped-up raves go on all night in the choicest South Beach venues. ◈ *Map R4 • Winter Party first 10 days in Mar; White Party late Nov*

4 Coconut Grove Arts Festival

The Grove *(see pp98–105)* comes fully alive with one of the biggest arts festivals in the country, complete with competitions, all-day concerts, tasty street food, and throngs of avid arts lovers. ◈ *Map G3 • 3rd weekend in Feb*

5 Miami-Dade County Fair and Exposition

A traditional American county fair, replete with rides, side-shows, cotton candy, candied apples, live performances, and exhibits relating to farm life and crafts. ◈ *Tamiami Park, Coral Way & SW 112th Ave, West Dade • for 18 days from 3rd Thu in Mar*

Carnaval Miami

Key West also hosts delightful, if obscure, events such as conch-blowing and Hemingway Days – See p121

Key West Fantasy Fest

6 Miami-Bahamas Goombay Festival

Celebrating Coconut Grove's Bahamian heritage, with music, dance, and loads of fun. ◈ *Map G3 • Usually Jun*

7 King Mango Strut

A Coconut Grove spoof on the now-defunct Orange Bowl Parade. ◈ *Map G3 • Last week of Dec*

8 Hispanic Heritage Festival

This month-long Latino blast, comprises street parties, food festivals, films, music and dance performances, and even an Hispanic beauty pageant. ◈ *Throughout Miami-Dade County • Oct*

9 South Beach Wine and Food Festival

Celebrating the talents of renowned wine producers and local and guest chefs. ◈ *www.sobewineandfoodfestival.com • late Feb*

10 International Mango Festival

The luscious fruit is celebrated with gusto. Enjoy a complete mango feast and learn how to tell when one is ripe. ◈ *Fairchild Tropical Gardens • Map G4 • 2nd weekend of Jul*

Top 10 Ethnic Attractions

1 Little Havana
A little slice of Cuba *(see pp14–15).*

2 Little Managua
Nicaraguan shops abound in the zone (also called Sweetwater) west of Calle Ocho.

3 Little Haiti
Come to check out a quirky botánica or two *(see pp91).*

4 Billie Swamp Safari Wildlife Center
The Seminole didactic style is "laugh & learn" *(see p29).*

5 Ah-Tah-Thi-Ki Museum
Exhibits on camp life, ceremonies, and the Seminole economy *(see p29).*

6 Miccosukee Indian Village
Basket-weaving, palmetto doll-making, beadwork, dugout carving, and alligator wrestling. ◈ *25 miles west of Florida Turnpike • 9am–5pm daily • Adm*

7 Overtown Historic Village
The African-American neighborhood has restored some historic buildings such as Dorsey House, at 250 NW 9th St.

8 Lyric Theater
Now a reborn venue for African-American cultural events. ◈ *819 NW 2nd Ave, Overtown*

9 Liberty City
Site of deadly race riots in 1980, this African-American neighborhood has many interesting murals and graffiti-inspired art.

10 Historic Homestead Museum and Around
Most of the historic downtown area has been restored – get a map from the museum. ◈ *41-43 North Krome Ave*

Left **Lowe Art Museum** Center **Wolfsonian Museum** Right **Historical Museum**

🔟 Museums

1 Lowe Art Museum
Undoubtedly Miami's top art museum, featuring extraordinary works from European, American, Chinese, Pre-Columbian, and Native American cultures *(see pp20–21).*

2 The Wolfsonian
The perfect complement to the unique Deco District, this is a museum and design research institute with over 70,000 modern design exhibits *(see pp22–3).*

3 Bass Museum of Art
A collection of Western fine art and design, and historical pictures of Miami Beach *(see p71).*

4 Norton Museum of Art
One of South Florida's finest, its European collection displays works by Rembrandt, Goya, Renoir, and Picasso. Americans include O'Keeffe and Pollock, and the museum also has strong ancient Chinese and Pre-Columbian collections. ◈ *1451 S Olive Ave, West Palm Beach • Map D2 • 561-832-5196 • www.norton.org • 10am–5pm Tue–Sat, noon–5pm Sun • Adm*

5 Miami Art Museum
Besides impressive temporary shows, MAM's collection focuses on art since the 1940s, and includes works by Frankenthaler, Gottleib, Rauschenberg, and Stella. ◈ *101 W Flagler St • Map M2 • 305-375-3000 • www.miamiartmuseum.org • 10am–5pm Tue–Fri, noon–5pm Sat–Sun • Adm*

6 World Erotic Art Museum
An amazing $10 million collection of erotic art from around the world. ◈ *Mezzanine level 1205 Washington Avenue • Map R4 • 305-532-9336 • 11am–midnight daily • Adm*

7 Historical Museum of Southern Florida
Starting as far back in prehistory as 10,000 years, the museum slips swiftly through the millennia

Left **Bass Museum of Art** Right **Norton Museum of Art**

Miami Art Museum

to reach Spanish colonization, Seminole culture, extravagance in the "Roaring Twenties," and Cuban immigration in more recent years. ❧ 101 West Flagler St • Map N2 • 305-375-1492 • www.historical-museum.org • 10am–5pm Mon–Sat (til 9pm Thu), noon–5pm Sun • Adm

8 Jewish Museum of Florida

With its stained-glass windows (one in memory of gangster Meyer Lansky) and Deco details, the synagogue itself is as fascinating as the exhibits it houses. The 230-year Jewish presence in Florida is amply covered. ❧ 301 Washington Ave., South Beach • Map R5 • 305-672-5044 • www.jewishmuseum.com • 10am–5pm Tue–Sun • Adm

9 Ah-Tah-Thi-Ki Museum

This excellent museum features Seminole artifacts, such as pottery and beautiful clothing. The Green Corn Ceremony is explained also, including the games, music, dance, and costumes involved. Outside, a nature trail leads through the cypress canopy, where signs explain the use of certain flora in Seminole culture (see p29).

10 Mel Fisher Maritime Museum

The romance of long-lost, booty-laden shipwrecks (see p117).

Top 10 Contemporary Collections

1 Rubell Family Collection
About 1,000 works by modern artists, including Haring, Koons, Basquiat, and Cuban artist José Bedia. ❧ 95 NW 29th St

2 Margulies Collection
Important photography collection, favoring straight-forward portraiture. ❧ 591 NW 27th St

3 Ambrosino Gallery
Work by artists Pablo Soria, William Cordova, and Barbara Strasen. ❧ 771 NE 125th St

4 Kevin Bruk Gallery, Miami
Featuring work by New York artists Max Gimblett and John Yau. ❧ 2249 NW 1st Place

5 Bernice Steinbaum Gallery, Miami
The work of Edouard Duval Carrie and Wendy Wischer. ❧ 3550 N. Miami Ave

6 Artspace/Virginia Miller Galleries
US and Latin American photographers and artists. ❧ 169 Madeira Ave, Coral Gables

7 Locust Projects
Specializing in computer-aided and video work by local artists. ❧ 105 NW 23rd St

8 Barbara Gillman Gallery
Showcasing the work of selected young local artists. ❧ 2320 N. Miami Ave

9 Cernuda Arte
Cuban art from all periods. ❧ 3155 Ponce de Leon Blvd, Coral Gables

10 Fredric Snitzer Gallery
New collage paintings, featuring the work of Sandy Winters. ❧ 2247 NW 1st Place

Left **Coral Castle** Center **Spanish Monastery** Right **Opa-Locka**

Historic Sites and Monuments

1 Vizcaya
James Deering's opulent monument celebrating Western civilization and its rich artistic traditions has become Miami's most beloved social and cultural center *(see pp16–17)*.

2 Ancient Spanish Monastery
Originally built in 1133–41 in Segovia, Spain, this monastic building was bought by William Randolph Hearst in 1925 and shipped to New York. The parts were eventually reassembled here in 1952, though, curiously, a few pieces were left over *(see p91)*.

3 The Barnacle
Built in 1891, this is Dade County's oldest house, which cleverly uses ship-building techniques to make it storm proof as well as comfortable (without the use of air-conditioning) in Florida's steamy climate *(see p100)*.

4 Coral Gables Merrick House
The house where the Merrick family lived in the late 1800s and where George Merrick, Coral Gables' master builder, grew up. The contrast between the modest surroundings of his home and the spectacle of his grandiose dreams is fascinating *(see pp18–19)*.

5 Coral Castle
This monument to unrequited love speaks volumes about early Florida's place in US history as a refuge for misfits, eccentrics, and visionaries. Land was cheap (the creator of Coral Castle bought his acre plot for $12 in 1920) and the population was sparse, so it was easy to do your own thing without being bothered. But how this gargantuan folly was actually constructed remains an enigma *(see p107)*.

6 Brigade 2506 Memorial
Little Havana's Eternal Flame and monument garden remembers those who died in the Bay of Pigs debacle, attempting to reclaim Cuba from leftist revolutionary forces in 1961 *(see p14)*.

7 Holocaust Memorial
Miami has one of the largest populations of Holocaust survivors in the world, so this stunning monument has extra poignancy. Sculpted by Kenneth Treister and finished in 1990, the centerpiece is an enormous bronze forearm bearing a stamped number from Auschwitz. The arm is thronged with nearly 100 life-sized figures in attitudes of suffering. The surrounding plaza has a graphic pictorial history of the Holocaust, and a granite wall listing the names of thousands of

Holocaust Memorial

For Miami's historic Art Deco District **See pp10–13**

concentration camp victims.
- *1933-45 Meridian Ave, South Beach*
- *305-538-1663 • www.holocaustmmb.org*

8 Opa-Locka
Despite the rather seamy area it inhabits, "The Baghdad of Dade County" is worth visiting for its 90 or so Moorish-style buildings. They were built here by Glenn Curtiss during the 1920s boom *(see p91).*

9 Charles Deering Estate
James Deering's half-brother built this winter residence for himself on Biscayne Bay. The original 19th-century house, Richmond Cottage, was destroyed by Hurricane Andrew in 1992, but it's been rebuilt and the entire estate refurbished since then, including the extraordinary Mediterranean-Revival mansion *(see p107).*

Stranaham House

10 Stranahan House
Fort Lauderdale's oldest house, built originally in 1901 as a trading post for the Seminoles. The handsome two-story riverside house is furnished with period antiques, but it is the photos that best evoke the past, such as Stranahan trading alligator hides, otter pelts, and egret plumes with the local Seminoles. Such prizes were brought in from the Everglades in dugout canoes.
- *335 SE 6th Ave., near Las Olas • Map 3 • 954-524-4736 • Adm*

Top 10 Historical Movers and Shapers

1 William Brickell
One of the first men to take advantage of the Homestead Act of 1862.

2 Henry M. Flagler
The legal mastermind (1830–1913) who opened up Florida through railroads and luxury construction.

3 Governor Napoleon Bonaparte Broward
Elected in 1905, he enacted Florida's first conservation laws and also a program for draining the Everglades.

4 Carl Fisher
An energetic developer in the early 1900s, Fisher was the first visionary owner of Miami Beach.

5 George Merrick
The imaginative mind behind the development of Coral Gables *(see pp18–19).*

6 The Deering Brothers
James and Charles built homes that are now major attractions *(see p16–17 & 107).*

7 Marjory Stoneman Douglas
The first of Florida's environmentalists, who single-handedly saved the Everglades. She died in 1998, at the age of 108.

8 Barbara Capitman
The driving force behind the movement to save the Art Deco hotels *(see p13).*

9 Julia Tuttle
The dynamic pioneer who convinced Henry Flagler to extend his railroad down to Miami, in 1896.

10 Chief Jim Billie
Controversial Seminole chief who brought wealth to his tribe in the 1980s, by building casinos on reservations.

Left **Deco Detail** Center **Mural Detail, Buick Building** Right **Mural, The Society of the Four Arts**

TOP 10 Architectural Wonders

1 Deco District
A national treasure of uplifting architecture. In saving it, South Miami Beach not only transformed itself but also inspired a national movement to preserve historic structures *(see pp10–13)*.

2 Biltmore Hotel and Coral Gables Congregational Church
Facing each other across lush, manicured gardens, these two structures are the heart of George Merrick's contribution to "The City Beautiful" *(see pp99 & 103)*.

3 Freedom Tower
Inspired by the famous belfry (formerly, under the Moors, a minaret for a mosque) of Seville's vast Cathedral. A museum is located in the lobby *(see p83)*.

Ingraham insignia

4 Granada Gate
A George Merrick fantasy, with references to Spanish-Moorish architecture, in this case nodding to the Alhambra in the Iberian mountain town of Granada. ◈ *Granada Blvd at the north entrance to Coral Gables*

5 Ingraham Building
This Renaissance-Revival beauty is a don't-miss landmark in Downtown Miami, and it evokes all the glamour of the 1920s' boom era *(see p85)*.

6 Bank of America Tower, International Place
I. M. Pei's striking take on the ziggurat theme so often used in Art Deco, looking for all the world like a stepped stack of CDs in various sizes. It's especially appealing at night when it's lit up with vibrant colors *(see p84)*.

7 Atlantis Condominium
Built by Arquitectonica in 1982 and soon thereafter one of the stars of *Miami Vice*, this "building with the hole in it" is in danger of being overrun by the rampant construction going on along Brickell. The "hole" is an ingenious 37-ft (11-m) cube cut out of the building's center, at the 12th floor. A red spiral staircase and a palm tree draw your attention to it in a delightful way ◈ *2025 Brickell Ave, Miami*

Biltmore Hotel

Freedom Tower

8 Estefan Enterprises

Also by Arquitectonica, this playful building takes the frivolity of Deco several steps further. A free-form green-wave tower slices through a cool blue cube, at once evoking both sea and sky, while colorful dancing flotsam seem to inhabit the green wave. The roof is an oasis, with sprouting trees. ⊗ *420 Jefferson Ave, Miami Beach*

9 Plymouth Congregational Church

This beautiful Mission-style edifice was built in 1916, though its massive door did come from a 17th-century monastery in the Pyrenees. ⊗ *3400 Devon Road, at Main Highway, Coconut Grove*

10 Key West Old Town

Key West *(see pp26–7)* has the largest collection of 19th-century structures in the US. About 4,000 buildings, mostly houses, embody the distinctive local style. Many architectural features take their cues from elements used on ships, such as roof hatches to allow air circulation. One unique innovation is the "eyebrow" house, with second-floor windows hidden under a front porch roof overhang, providing shade in the unremitting heat.

Top 10 Murals and Mosaics

1 Buick Building
Murals adorn the building's east and west walls. While there, enjoy the amazing public art in the Design District. ⊗ *3841 NE 2nd Ave*

2 The Netherland
Fantastic mural of indolent sunbathers. ⊗ *1330 Ocean Drive, South Beach*

3 Bacardi Import Headquarters
You can't miss the tropical foliage mosaic. Be sure to notice the building next to it, too. ⊗ *2100 Biscayne Blvd*

4 Miami Beach Post Office
The classy Deco entrance has a triptych mural of Ponce de Leon and the Native American peoples. ⊗ *1300 Washington Ave, South Beach*

5 Coral Gables City Hall
Denman Fink created the mural on the bell tower. The one above the stairs is by John St. John. ⊗ *405 Biltmore Way*

6 Little Havana
A series of seven quirky murals. ⊗ *Calle Ocho 1507–13*

7 Office Building
A 1940s mural depicting labor, the arts, and the Universe. ⊗ *1617 Drexel Ave, South Beach*

8 The Society of the Four Arts
Allegorical murals from 1939. ⊗ *Four Arts Plaza, Palm Beach*

9 Wyland Whaling Walls
An undersea world of whales and other cetaceans. ⊗ *201 William St, Key West*

10 Bahama Village
Charming mural evoking the simplicity and beauty of Caribbean life. ⊗ *Thomas St at Petronia St*

Left **Coral Castle** Center **Botánica sign** Right **Perky's Bat Tower**

Offbeat Places

1 Coral Castle

A lovesick Latvian immigrant's valentine to the girl back home who spurned him. These bizarre monoliths form one of the area's oddest monuments, yet it is strangely touching nevertheless (see p44).

2 Alhambra Water Tower, Coral Gables

Resembling a plump lighthouse, this colorful tower (built 1924) was the work of Denman Fink, George Merrick's uncle. Neglected for decades, it was fully restored in 1993 and, although no longer used, the tower's elegant Moorish touches make it an intriguing piece of industrial architecture. ◈ Alhambra Circle, at Ferdinand St and Greenway Ct

Alhambra Water Tower

3 Ermita de la Caridad Church, Coconut Grove

Built in 1966 on the edge of Biscayne Bay, this peculiar conical church draws in Miami's Cuban exiles. The altar is oriented toward Cuba, rather than to the east, and above it is a mural depicting the history of the Catholic Church in Cuba. The shrine is dedicated to the Virgin of Charity, the Cuban patron saint. ◈ 3609 S Miami Ave, Coconut Grove

4 Opa-Locka

Another delightful example of the quirky fantasy architecture dreamed up in the 1920s. Unfortunately, the run-down area around is anything but a dream (see p45).

5 South Beach Lifeguard Huts

In all the world, it is unlikely that you'll find any lifeguard huts so aesthetically pleasing as these Deco-style delights (see p11).

6 Santería and Vodou Botánicas

South Florida at its most darkly exotic. The botánicas (shops) carry all sorts of magic potions and power objects used in the practice of the hybrid religions of Santería and Vodou (voodoo) – a little Roman Catholicism mixed with a lot of ancient West African ritual and belief (see p15).

Ermita de la Caridad Church

South Beach lifeguard hut

7 Stiltsville, Key Biscayne

Drive to the southernmost tip of Key Biscayne, look way out on the water, and you'll spy six lonesome structures built on stilts. These fishermen's bungalows are the last of what was once quite a community. Their number has dwindled considerably due to hurricanes and legal squabbles. ✎ *Map H4*

8 Perky's Bat Tower, Sugarloaf Key

In 1929 one Richter C. Perky, a property speculator, built this awkward structure, designed to be every bat's dream-home; in exchange, the bats were supposed to rid the area of its voracious mosquitoes. Unfortunately, the bats he imported instantly flew away, while the mosquitoes thrived. ✎ *MM 17, nr Sugarloaf Lodge*

9 Nancy's Secret Garden, Key West

Imagine entering a timeless world, full of humor and a funky, indefinable Key West aura *(see p37)*.

10 "The Garden of Eden," Key West

Devoted nudists can find an appreciative milieu in this bar *(see p124)*, as they can within the walls and gardens of many guesthouses around town. ✎ *The Bull, third floor 224 Duval St, Key West*

Top 10 Scandals

1 Barbara Meller-Jensen, Hapless Tourist
The unwary German visitor was murdered in 1993, tarnishing Miami's tourism image.

2 Laroche, Orchid Thief
In 1997, Laroche was fined for poaching with the aid of Native American Seminoles, who are exempt from the law.

3 Versace's Murder
Andrew Cunanan shot the fashion magnate on his front steps on July 15, 1997.

4 Mrs. Jeb Bush
The Florida governor's wife was caught with $19,000 of undeclared couture in 1999.

5 Elián González Standoff
The repatriation of a Cuban boy at gunpoint by the US Justice Dept hit the world's media in 2000 and tore the Cuban community here apart.

6 Presidential Election Debacle
Florida became the epicenter of the election in 2000, with the result anything but clear.

7 Estefan Lawsuits
In 2001, Cubana singer Gloria Estefan was rocked by a claim that her husband, Emilio, had sexually harassed another man.

8 Miss Cleo, TV-Telephone Psychic
2002 saw the collapse of the psychic hotline that didn't employ "genuine" psychics.

9 Bishop O'Connell's Fall from Grace
Casualty of a "topical storm" over pedophilia in 2002.

10 Rosie O'Donnell
In 2002, the talk-show hostess came out as a lesbian and championed gay adoptions in the only state to ban them.

Left **Lincoln Road Mall** Center **Hollywood Broadwalk** Right **Van Dyke Café**

Spots for People-Watching

1 Ocean Drive
The epitome of the "American Riviera." Sit in a café, or cruise up and down the strip in a convertible, on skates, or simply on foot. And, of course, if you've got it – the buff bod, golden tan, and all – Ocean Drive is the place to show it off *(see p8)*.

Ocean Drive

2 CocoWalk
A host of select shops, restaurants, outdoor cafés, and a cineplex provides the entertainment. But, here in the heart of the Grove, it's great just to hang out and listen to the live band playing most of the time on the balcony above *(see p100)*.

3 Bayside Marketplace
Never a dull moment in Downtown Miami's hottest daytime spot, featuring boutiques, live music, street performers, and ethnic dining right on the marina *(see p83)*.

4 Lincoln Road Mall
Second only to Ocean Drive in its star-quality appeal. Lined with sculpture-fountains and plants, this pedestrian area with its outdoor eateries is always lively. Score, at No. 727, is very good after dark *(see p57)*.

5 Terrace at the Tides
Try the famous Tropical Popsicle Martini as you watch the people go by. Popular with celebrities, look around, you might be dining side by side with the rich and famous *(see p78)*.

6 Clevelander
This hotel's daytime beach-front cafés evolve into one of SoBe's top pool-bar scenes after dark. Its proximity to the beach inspires a more casual style than the usual nightspots, and there's always a crowd to enjoy happy hour and live music *(see p78)*.

7 The Forge
A 70-year institution and a perennial favorite with celebrities such as Madonna and Michael Jordan. There are atmospheric themed rooms, such as the Library, and the overall mood is cozy and

Coco Walk

Clevelander

romantic. The menu favors old-fashioned staples, like steaks and chocolate soufflé, and there's a formidable wine cellar. ◈ *432 Arthur Godfrey Rd (41st St), Miami Beach • 305-538-8533 • \$\$\$\$\$*

8 Commodore Plaza
Coconut Grove's second most frequented spot is this intersection, where every corner features a top viewing position for the constant circulation of pedestrian traffic, everyone scoping out a café or restaurant, and each other. Try the Green Street Café *(see p102)*.

9 Hollywood Broadwalk
A rare swath of beach where a 2.5-mile (4-km) pedestrian walkway fronts directly on the sand, just to the north of Miami Beach. It's non-stop surfside fun all the way, with loads of revelers all kinds cruising up and down *(see p24)*.

10 Mallory Square, Key West
Especially at sunset, this huge square at the Gulf end of Duval Street is a gathering place for all sorts of locals and visitors. Street performers keep it lively, and there are plenty of vendors of food and souvenirs *(see p26)*.

Sunset at Mallory Square

Top 10 Trendy Cafés

1 News Café
Justifiably SoBe's most famous café *(see p8)*.

2 Van Dyke Café
Lincoln Road's top draw, both day and night, including a wraparound balcony and a jazz club *(see p78)*.

3 Green Street Café
Coconut Grove's numero uno for people-watching, happy hour, and creative meals *(see p102)*.

4 Café Tu Tu Tango
One of the most popular cafés in Coconut Grove. Located on the second floor of the CocoWalk Mall, over-looking the city *(see p102)*.

5 Paninoteca
A wonderful place to sit and sip a drink, or to enjoy a superb pizza or salad you're invited to design yourself. ◈ *809 Lincoln Rd, S Beach & 264 Miracle Mile, Coral Gables*

6 Mango's Tropical Café
One of the hottest action venues on South Beach – live music and dancing, Floribbean dishes, and free-flowing cocktails *(see p78)*.

7 The Clay Hotel
This beautiful period building is now a youth hostel, so its modest café is always thronged with international youth *(see p152)*.

8 Books and Books
Don't let the quietness deceive you, this is a very happening place *(see p104)*.

9 11th Street Diner
One of the most popular eateries, especially with the gay crowd *(see p79)*.

10 Mangoes, Key West
A restaurant, bar, and sidewalk café, located on a busy corner *(see p125)*.

Left **The beach at 12th Street, SoBe** Right **Cathode Ray, Fort Lauderdale**

🔟 Gay and Lesbian Venues

1 Beach at 12th Street, SoBe

While all of South Beach is a gay haven, this particular stretch is where the guys tend to gather in their imposing, thong-clad throngs. ✪ Map S3–4

2 Haulover Park Beach, Miami Beach

Transvestites

Keep walking north, past the straight nude beach, and you'll soon reach the gay section – where no heavy action is tolerated. ✪ Map H3

3 Fort Lauderdale Gay Beaches

There are two major beaches "Where the Boys Are" in the Fort Lauderdale area: the stretch where Sebastian Street meets A1A; and John U. Lloyd State Park Beach. You'll know you've reached there when you sight guys with pumped muscles and skimpy swimsuits. ✪ Map D3

4 Gay and Lesbian Community Center of South Florida

Located in very gay Wilton Manors, this is a big and well-maintained center. There's an extensive library of gay literature and reference works, friendly staff, a full calendar of special events, and plenty of opportunities for lively social interaction. ✪ 1717 N Andrews Ave • 954-463-9005

5 Cathode Ray, Fort Lauderdale

This is the place to be in downtown Fort Lauderdale, especially when all the white-collar guys show up after work to relax and unwind during happy hour (2–8pm). There's a comedy night on Mondays, and the weekend high-energy partying culminates with big-screen viewing of *Queer as Folk*. ✪ 1307 East Las Olas Blvd • 954-462-8611

6 Shoppes of Wilton Manors, Fort Lauderdale

An entire gay shopping mall! Shops here include Gay Mart, In the Pink Books, Oh What a Basket, Greetings from the Rainbow, Inside Out Boutique, and Wicked Leather. There are also many prominent bars, gyms, clubs, and restaurants, such as Around the World Pizza, Chardees, and Simply Delish. ✪ 2200 block of Wilton Drive

7 Georgie's Alibi, Fort Lauderdale

This is a video bar, café, and sports bar, located in Fort Lah-Dee-Dah's unique gay shopping center, in its unique gay town – Wilton Manors – which even has its own gay mayor. The Alibi opened in April of 1997 in a then rundown area, but Wilton Manors has since blossomed into a thriving gay

*The best of SoBe's gay and lesbian venues are on **p76***

Wilton Manors, Fort Lauderdale

community, and this bar has flourished with it. In fact, the Alibi is one of South Florida's best gay venues, and always worth checking out. ◈ 2266 Wilton Drive, Wilton Manors • 954-565-2526 • www.georgiesalibi.com

8 Coliseum, Fort Lauderdale

A newer incarnation of a former straight venue, this place is fresh and youthful, featuring lavish drag acts and an abundance of beautiful young musclemen. Every night some of the area's better-known DJs launch global groove house music "dance-a-thongs". ◈ 2520 S Miami Road • 954-832-0100 • www.coliseumnightclub.com

9 Boardwalk, Fort Lauderdale

A huge gay nightclub that attracts big crowds of all ages throughout the week. It is a vibrant and popular place, with dancers performing every night. On Wednesdays an amateur dance contest known as the "New Meat Contest" is held, while Thursday night is towel night. Drag shows are put on at the weekends. The happy hour is from 3pm to 9pm and on Sundays there is a barbecue from 5pm. ◈ 1721 North Andrews Ave • 954-463-6969

10 Gay and Lesbian Community Center, Key West

Set on an appealing square, the center offers a library, a lounge, and all the information you might need. Pluses include a monthly calendar of special events, such as wine-and-cheese parties, discussion groups, and a film series. Free anonymous HIV testing is available, or just stop by for advice and a chat. ◈ Map A6 • 524 Truman Ave • 305-292-3223 • www.glcckeywest.org

Beach at Fort Lauderdale

For exclusively gay and lesbian accommodations See p153

Left **Worth Avenue** Right **Collins and 7th Street, SoBe**

TOP 10 Chic Shopping Centers

1 Bal Harbour Shops
The ultimate in chi-chi, down to the English spelling of "Harbour" (see p92). Here are Hermès, Gucci, Armani, Dior, Bulgari, Tiffany, Versace, and Louis Vuitton, not to mention Chanel, Dolce & Gabbana, Prada, and Lalique. Need we say more? Well, okay, Nieman Marcus, and Saks Fifth Avenue. ✆ 9700 Collins Avenue • Map H2 • 954-760-4005 • www.balharbourshops.com

Gucci emblem

2 Village of Merrick Park
The brand-new Village of Merrick Park offers luxury retail stores, set amid an immaculate urban garden ideal for concerts. Neiman Marcus and Miami's very first Nordstrom are at its heart, along with a range of fine shops and places to eat, such as the elegant Palm Restaurant. The Mediterranean-Revival style, with landscaped walkways and fountains, is in keeping with the precedent set by the city's founder George Merrick (see pp18–19). ✆ Miracle Mile, Coral Gables

3 Collins and 7th Street, SoBe
For your upscale shopping convenience, all the SoBe boutiques that seriously matter are clustered around this intersection. ✆ Map R4

4 The Falls
Semi-open-air arcades with waterfalls and tropical vegetation form the backdrop to over 100 shops. Mostly upscale, they include Bloomingdale's, Macy's, Banana Republic, the Pottery Barn, and the Discovery Channel Store for kids. In addition, there are 12 movie screens and some 13 restaurants and cafés, including the inevitable Haagen Däzs and Mrs. Field's Cookies. ✆ 8888 SW 136th St. • 305-255-4570 • www.shopthefalls.com

5 Aventura Mall
Bloomingdale's and Macy's are the upscale anchors here, in addition to specialty stores including Abercrombie & Fitch, Ann Taylor, Guess?, J. Crew, Everything But Water, Fossil, and Clinique. Art galleries, some

Aventura Mall

excellent restaurants, an international food court, and a 24-screen cineplex complete the picture. ◈ Biscayne Blvd & 196th St, Aventura • 305-935-1110 • www.shop aventuramall.com

Boca Raton

6 Dadeland Mall

Fear not! There is a Saks Fifth Avenue even way down in South Miami – plus some 170 high-end specialty shops and several other fine anchor stores, including Florida's largest Macy's. Unless you're shopping on the cheap, just ignore the fact that there's also a JC Penney, a Radio Shack, and a Best Buy. The décor is pleasing, if a bit predictable – palm-tree pillars and ceilings painted to resemble skies. ◈ 7535 N Kendall Drive • 305-665-6226 • www.simon.com

7 Worth Avenue, Palm Beach

Loads of marvelously expensive, ultra-exclusive must-haves for the crème of the haves (see p25).

8 Las Olas Boulevard and the Galleria

Fort Lauderdale's high-end shopping is spread between its main street downtown and a mall just near the beach. Las Olas' 100-plus boutiques are unique, all mixed with some really good restaurants. The Galleria, East Sunrise Blvd at A1A, offers Neiman Marcus and Saks Fifth Avenue.

9 Boca Raton

Newly expanded, Boca's premier mall just took a quantum leap into even greater luxury. It now has a Nordstrom to go with

its Saks, Cartier, Tiffany, Bloomie's, and Williams-Sonoma. Set amid exotic foliage, skylights, hand-glazed tiles, and sculptural accents, there's also a fancy cuisine court – no fast-food chain joints here! If you venture into downtown Boca, be sure to stroll through pastel-pink Mizner Park, where you'll also find more chic shopping options. ◈ Town Center 6000 W Glades Road • 561-368-6000 • www.simon.com

10 Duval Street, Key West

Besides the tacky T-shirt shops, Key West's main drag (see p26) is also home to some superb emporiums of quality merchandise, including: clothing at Fast Buck Freddie's (No. 500); Sunlion Jewelry (No. 513); Island Furniture and Accessories (No. 1024); Gingerbread Square Gallery, mixing local artists and world-class glass blowers (No. 1207); and Archeo Ancient Art, which specializes in African art and Persian rugs (No. 1208).

For the best individual shops around Miami and the Keys
See pp75, 88, 94, 104, 110 & 122

Left **Ceramic Art Deco buildings** Center **South Beach boutique** Right **Española Way**

🔟 Malls and Markets

Bayside Marketplace

1 Bayside Marketplace

This sprawling marketplace abounds with chain boutiques, the occasional trendy local shop adding spice. *(see p83)*.

2 Sawgrass Mills Mall

This claims to be the largest shopping center in the world, a boast you'll believe as you drive its circumference trying to find the way in. This 8-acre (3-ha) mercantile behemoth comprises more than 300 discount outlets, from top-of-the-line goods to bargain basement rejects.
🅂 *12801 W Sunrise Blvd, at Flamingo Rd*
• *1-800-356-4557*

3 Seybold Building

Located just off Flagler Street, where all sorts of cut-rate electronics can be haggled

over, this building specializes in gems and jewelry, both wholesale and retail. Mainly a place for jewelers to pick up stock, ordinary mortals, too, can rummage the sparklers and invest in either loose gems or unique pieces of fine jewelry. 🅂 *36 NE 1st St*
• *305-374-7922*

4 Dolphin Mall

More than 200 stores fill Greater Miami's newest middle-range mall. In part, this is an outlet for such heavy hitters as Saks Fifth Avenue, Brooks Brothers, Giorgio's et al., but there is also a host of boutiques as well as a 19-screen cineplex at the heart of it all, on the "Ramblas", where the liveliest eateries are found.
🅂 *11401 NW 12th Street* • *305-365-7446*
• *www.shopdolphinmall.com*

5 Dania Beach Historic Antiques District

Dolphin Mall

Here is South Florida's largest concentration of antiques shops. More than 100 dealers offer an array of furniture, fine art, and jewelry, as well as glass, pottery and china, and various other collectibles. Prices vary greatly, so shop around for bargains.
🅂 *Federal Highway 1 north for two blocks from Dania Beach Blvd*

Antiques District

6 Española Way Market
On Saturday and Sunday, there's a small, rather esoteric market along here, selling flowers, arts and crafts, and organic products. An array of vaguely hippie items make an appearance, such as amulets, scented candles, stones, oriental bric-a-brac, and exotic clothing – all natural, of course. You can get your palm read, too, or decorated with henna if you prefer. 🔊 *15th St, South Beach • Map R3*

7 Los Pinareños Fruteria
Little Havana's foremost fruit and veg market, and you can get fresh juice, snacks, and flowers, too *(see p88).*

8 Opa-Locka/Hialeah Flea Market
Up to 1,200 dealers show up here seven days a week from 7am–7pm, hawking everything and anything you can think of to satisfy an orgy of acquisition. Weekends are best, when the number of dealers, browsers, and bargain-hunters swells. 🔊 *12705 NW 47th Ave*

9 Lincoln Road Markets
This lively pedestrian area, graced with attractive fountains and upscale restaurants and shops, also offers various markets. On Sunday, there's one selling fruit and flowers, plus regional products, and specialties. Every other Sunday from October to May, there's also a collectors' market, and on the second Tuesday of the month "Arts on the Road" features all sorts of work. 🔊 *Lincoln Road, between Washington Ave and Alton Rd • Map Q–R2*

10 The Swap Shop
Eighty-eight acres (35 ha) of shopping at bargain prices serving 12 million shoppers a year. The outdoor flea market features antiques, collectibles, clothing, plants, and a farmers' market. In total there are some 2,000 vendors. Inside, in addition to an international food court and a video arcade, there are also amusement rides. The complex also claims the world's largest drive-in theater with 14 screens. 🔊 *3291 W Sunrise Blvd, between I-95 & Florida's Turnpike, Fort Lauderdale • www.floridaswapshop.com*

Lincoln Road market

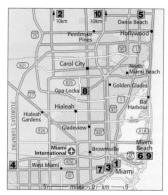

Left **Mynt** Center **Jazid** Right **Pearl Champagne Bar at Penrod's Complex**

🔟 Nightlife

crobar

1 crobar
Housed in an architectural gem, the former Cameo Theater, this is high-tech fun at its most cutting-edge. crobar is glitzy and full of attitude, and you should definitely wear your Prada bowling shoes, or whatever's the latest thing to turn the fashion cognoscenti's heads (see p77).

2 Jazid
A special place in Miami Beach for those who appreciate jazz. South Florida's top musicians perform nightly. Since there's no cover, do the right thing and order a drink or two to make sure this haven of anti-chic stays afloat. You're there for the music, the real thing in a sea of glamorous SoBe hype (see p77).

3 Mansion
One of the hottest clubs on South Beach. Sweeping staircases, ornate fireplaces, exposed brick walls, and towering arches feature throughout. There are cozy corners and private rooms for groups. A place to see and be seen (see p77).

4 B.E.D.
Mixed gay and straight clientele, famous food, and, yes, beds, and only beds, for dining on or for flopping when you take a break from bopping. Gimmicky it may be, but devotees say it's "just the right mix of weird and wonderful" (see p77).

5 Opium Garden
Where you could very well rub elbows with a celebrity or two, if you can get in. At its peak of recherché cachet at the time of writing, it's popularity with the big-name stars is bound to wane, but one visit will confirm its undeniable charms (see p77).

6 Bongos Cuban Café
Located in the American Airlines Arena in Miami, this nightspot has plenty of rhythm, music, and dancing. It was started by Gloria and Emilio Estefan and combines authentic Cuban cuisine and hot dance music. Professional dancers get the crowd going (see p77).

Mansion nightclub

South Beach is the focus of Miami's nightlife. For nightlife in the Keys See pp123–4

Beach party at Penrod's Complex

7 Penrod's Complex
This beachfront complex is a playground for the Euro-hip and trendy denizens of SoBe. Nikki Beach is located on the first floor and Pearl Restaurant & Champagne Lounge is on the second. New themes and dances every week, fashion shows, and interactive entertainment. Valet parking (see p77).

8 Mynt
Enjoy a menu of custom cocktails at this hot nightspot in South Beach. The hippy crowd here enjoy partying in style (see p77).

9 Twist
SoBe's premier gay venue, huge and always jumping, but it doesn't get started until very late, of course, and then it goes till dawn. Don't show before midnight unless you want to be considered a desperate wallflower. So popular of late that even straight people are beginning to take to it (see p76).

10 Tantra Restaurant and Lounge
A water wall greets you when you step inside Tantra. Inhale the jasmine-scented candles while you listen to the new age music. There's always a line to get in, but don't go too early. The fun doesn't start until the small hours. (see p77).

Top 10 Tropical Tipples

1 Mojito
Papa Hemingway's favorite splash: light rum, crushed mint leaves, sugar, and lime to taste. Sublime!

2 Hurricane
For a howling success, mix dark and light rums, blue Curaçao, and lemon juice.

3 Piña Colada
The blend of coconut milk, pineapple juice, and a choice rum is impossible to beat.

4 Rum Runner
Shades of Prohibition-era Caribbean smugglers, this classic comes in many styles and fruity flavors: watermelon, grenadine, blackberry, etc.

5 Sangria
The variations of fruit in red wine are almost endless.

6 Cosmopolitan
Variations on this vodka and Cointreau theme are creative. Often done with cranberry and/or orange notes.

7 Daiquiri
Another timeless Caribbean rum concoction, any way you like it: mango, strawberry, lime, peach, guava, etc.

8 Margarita
Not neglecting this south-of-the-border treat, in regular and frozen incarnations, paired with any fruit – and a range of liqueurs, too.

9 Mai Tai
One version of the Polynesian perennial features crème de noyaux, banana, grenadine, and tropical juices.

10 Martini
Be prepared for this old standby to appear in a thousand creative guises: with unexpected fruit liqueurs, for example, or even with white or milk chocolate!

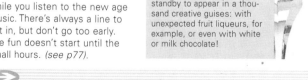

Left **Stone crab claws** Right **Tap Tap**

Restaurants

Norman's, Coral Gables

inventiveness without limits are the keynotes here, taste-bud awakening combinations of Oriental and local ingredients that will have you marveling at the chef's ingenuity *(see p79)*.

1 Norman's, Coral Gables
Haute-nouvelle-evolved fusion cuisine at its peak of foodie perfection. Norman has gained a much-deserved national and international reputation for his subtle inventiveness, and he's published a number of books revealing some, but not all, of his secrets *(see p105)*.

2 Mark's South Beach, South Beach
Another connoisseur's dream spot, just a block from the chicest beach in the US, at the Post-Modernized Hotel Nash. The setting is dreamy, to go with the artfully presented food *(see p79)*.

3 Pacific Time, South Beach
Lincoln Road's answer to fusion sublimity. Freshness and

4 Escopazzo, South Beach
As close to authentic Italian food as you're likely to get outside of the peninsula itself. It's more or less family style, so you'll feel like one of the regulars in this unpretentious little place *(see p79)*.

5 Tap Tap, South Beach
Colors and more colors greet the eye everywhere you look, most of it semi-religious imagery depicting various beneficent Voodoo gods and goddesses. Hearty, simple – and spicy – Haitian flavors stimulate the palate *(see p79)*.

6 Versailles, Little Havana
Everybody's favorite Cuban restaurant is an essential stop on a visit to Little Havana – a busy,

Left **Mark's South Beach** Right **Tap Tap interior**

Joe's Stone Crab

fairly rambunctious place. Cuban food tends to be a challenge to delicate digestive systems, but it's authentic *(see pp15 & 89)*.

7 Joe's Stone Crab, South Beach

A SoBe institution and always packed, despite being vast. Located right on the beach, it's always lots of fun and consistently excellent, although a bit too touristy for some *(see p79)*.

8 Café Tu Tu Tango, Coconut Grove

A friendly, engaging theme restaurant – real artists paint while you dine – that turns out light, nouvelle Floribbean food. Located in the Grove's groovy downtown CocoWalk complex, it's always bustling with good-looking 20- and 30-somethings *(see p105)*.

9 Monty's Stone Crab Seafood House and Raw Bar, Coconut Grove

Order a pile of peel-and-eat shrimp and a dollop or two of cocktail sauce, and seat yourself under a thatched breezeway while you shuck. Right on the water, near Coconut Grove's parks, it's one of the nicest places to have a casual meal *(see p105)*.

10 Cancun Grill, Miami Lakes

Exceptional Mexican cuisine at reasonable prices. This is the real thing, unpretentious and full of local color *(see p89)*.

Top 10 Floribbean Food and Drink

1 Café Cubano (Cafecito)
A tiny cup of intensely sweet, black coffee is the mainstay of life for many. If you want it with a drop of milk, ask for a *cortadito*.

2 Conch Chowder or Fritters
The snail- or slug-like creature that lives in beautiful pink shells is served up in a traditional, rather chewy dish.

3 Black Beans and Rice
"Moors and Christians" is the staple of the Cuban diet. Its savory, smoky flavor complements almost everything.

4 Yucca/Plantain Chips
The variations on bananas and potatoes are often served as deep-fried chips – slightly sweet and aromatic.

5 Blackened Grouper
Having your fish cooked "blackened" is a Cajun recipe that has caught on in most restaurants in South Florida.

6 Cevíche
A seafood marinade using lime juice, onions, green bell peppers, and cilantro (coriander).

7 Lechon Asado
Pork is a big part of the Cuban diet. This term translates as "roast suckling pig," and is the ultimate feast.

8 Chimichurri
A sauce with olive oil, garlic, lemon juice or wine vinegar, and parsley. Jalapeño peppers are optional.

9 Key Lime Pie
The Key lime looks more like a lemon but makes the most exquisite pie.

10 Alfajores
A typical Cuban pastry composed of chocolate, custard, and coconut.

For more great places to eat in Miami and the Keys
See pp79, 89, 95, 105, 111, 125 & 130

Left **Lifeguard hut on the Gold Coast** Center **Deco District** Right **Little Haiti, reached on Hwy 1**

Drives and Walks

Downtown Miami

1 Miami Beach to Tip of Key Biscayne

From South Beach, drive west on 5th Street, which becomes the MacArthur Causeway, I-395. Great views to be had over the water and the posh artificial islands, notably Star, Palm, and Hibiscus. Soon you'll be soaring over Downtown on the overpass that leads around to I-95, getting a bird's-eye view of the many skyscrapers, which are particularly attractive at night. Just before I-95 ends, take the exit for Key Biscayne. Stop at the Ricken-backer Causeway tollbooth ($1). The high arching road offers more great views of the skyline and takes you to deserted Virginia Key and then to quiet Key Biscayne. ◈ Map H3–4

2 Routes North

There are three ways to make your way by car north from Miami: Interstate 95 is the fastest, unless it's rush hour, but is really only to be used if you have a certain destination in mind. Highway 1 is closer to the sea, but is lined with local businesses practically all the way, so the stop-and-go traffic can be a real drag. A1A, however, makes the time spent decidedly worthwhile, rewarding the traveler with a range of natural beauty and elegant neighborhoods of the Gold and Treasure Coasts *(see pp24–5 & 128).*

3 Miami to Key West

You can do this drive in about three-and-a-half hours, but why hurry? There are great sights along the way, like the fantastic giant lobster at Treasure Village artists' colony. It's also definitely worth a stop to have a great sea-food lunch or dinner on the water. Other attractions include parks and nature preserves *(see pp36–7)*, and Perky's Bat Tower *(see p49)*. ◈ Map D4–A6

The Everglades

Tips for getting around Miami are on **p137**

SoBe hotels

4 Everglades Trails
There are several roads for exploring the Everglades: I-75, Alligator Alley; Hwy 41, the Tamiami Trail; or the less developed road (No. 9336) from Florida City. Off all of these roads, you'll find many opportunities for excursions into the wild *(see also pp28–9 & 127)*.

5 Deco District
With some 800 Tropical Deco wonders to behold, you can hardly miss; just walk or bike along Ocean Drive, and Collins and Washington Avenues between about 5th and 22nd Streets *(see also pp10–13)*.
✪ Map R5–S1

6 SoBe Streetlife
Almost synonymous with the Deco District. All the action is concentrated in three areas: Ocean Drive and the parallel streets of Collins and Washington (where most of the clubs are); the seductive Lincoln Road and the Española Way pedestrian malls *(see also pp8–9 & 57)*.

7 Calle Ocho
The main walking part of little Havana lies along SW 8th Street, between about 11th and 17th Avenues. But interesting spots are quite spread out for blocks around, and most of them are best found by driving, then exploring on foot *(see pp14–15)*.

8 Coco Village
Always lively, usually with young, perky people, this is downtown Coconut Grove. As well as shops, outdoor eateries, and cafés, live bands often play in CocoWalk *(see also pp98–105)*.

9 Key West Old Town
The only sensible way to get around Key West is either on foot or by bike; there's so much detail to take in and, besides, parking is usually a problem here. A planned tour can be fine *(see p121)*, but it's just as good to walk wherever inspiration leads *(see also pp26–7)*.

10 Palm Beach
To experience the essence of this wealthy community, begin your walk at Worth Ave. on the beach at Ocean Blvd. Walk west and check out as many of the fabulous shops as you dare. Continue on to Addison Mizner's pink palace, Casa de Leoni (No. 450), then take Lake Drive north to Royal Palm Way. Visit the Society of the Four Arts, then continue on north to the Flagler Museum. Finally, go east along Royal Poinciana Way and south to The Breakers *(see p25)*.

Mallory Square, Key West

Left **Fairchild Tropical Garden** Right **Hotel Place St. Michel**

Romantic Spots

1 Villa Vizcaya Gardens
A glorious pastiche of styles from more or less 500 years of European architecture, most of it bought in the Old World by an early 20th-century farm machinery magnate to be remodeled into this comfortable palace *(see pp16–17)*.

2 Venetian Pool
A lush fantasy of water, gardens, and sculpted stone, where Esther Williams (bathing-beauty diva of yesteryear) used to star in synchronized swimming movies. The pool was born of the mind of visionary entrepreneur George Merrick *(see pp18–19)*.

3 Ancient Spanish Monastery Cloister and Gardens
With its magnificent gardens and cloisters redolent of ancient lands and courtly love, this has become a popular spot for weddings. The building can be traced back to 12th-century Spain, though it didn't make its way to Florida

Ancient Spanish Monastery

until the 20th century. Having lain dormant in packing crates for years, it was finally reassembled in the 1950s *(see p91)*.

4 Fairchild Tropical Garden
The tranquil, silvery lakes, broad vistas and lush, dappled retreats are capable of bringing out the romantic in anyone. Badly damaged by Hurricane Andrew in 1992, the gardens have made a brilliant comeback, and are certainly worth a stroll to inhale the fragrant, shaded bowers, and perhaps stay for dinner at the nearby Red Fish Grill *(see also p107)*.

Venetian Pool

5 Coral Castle

One Edward Leedskalnin created this huge coral rock Valentine heart to win back his fickle love. She remained unmoved by his Herculean labors, however, and he died here alone in 1951 *(see also p107)*.

Morikami

6 Morikami Japanese Gardens

The 1,000-year-old originals of some of these deeply peaceful settings were designed for Japanese nobility – places of inspiration for them to recite poetry to each other, or to seek solace in troubled times. Few places evoke the serenity and spiritual depth you can sense here, in the silent rocks and the murmuring cascades *(see also p37)*.

7 Tantra

Aphrodisiac cuisine in an erotic arena evoke a sense of Indo-Persian culture. Real grass carpets and sensuous sculptures and paintings set the tone. Sublime Middle-Eastern and Indian fusion dishes are served in a somewhat desultory, yet suggestive, fashion in a candlelit ambience where palm fans softly spin. ◊ *1445 Pennsylvania Ave • 305-672-4765 • $$$$$*

8 Red Fish Grill

Perhaps the most starry-eyed setting in Miami, with its shimmering bay views and evocatively lighted foliage. The potent backdrop of Biscayne Bay, Fairchild Tropical Gardens, and nearby Mattheson Hammock Park and saltwater Atoll Pool make this an unforgettable place to dine. Attentive service and delicious food *(see p111)*.

9 Hotel Place St. Michel

French-style boutique hotel with an exquisite restaurant. Stay a night or two and you'll think you're in a chic little pension in Paris. The subtly lit bistro is a perfect place for a quietly intimate tête-à-tête, yet all this is within walking distance of downtown Coral Gables *(see also pp105 & 150)*.

10 Mallory Square, Key West, at sunset

Although you will most likely be there with a hoard of other sunset-viewers, the beauty of this moment and the general air of merriment will provide you with a memorable experience. Watch a tall ship sail in front of the huge setting sun, blazing orangy-pink at the Gulf's edge. True romantics should keep an eye out for the beguiling green flash that's said to occur just before the sun disappears below the horizon – if you catch it, it means good luck in love *(see also p26)*.

Left **Museum of Science and Planetarium** Right **Historical Museum of Southern Florida**

Children's Attractions

1 Parrot Jungle Island
This new $47-million theme park is conveniently located in the heart of Miami (see p71).

2 Hobie Beach
An excellent stretch of beach, popular not only with windsurfers but also with families appreciative of its calm, shallow waters (see pp30–31).

3 Miami Seaquarium
Lolita the killer whale, Flipper the movie-star dolphin, and Salty the sea lion are all on hand to thrill the kids (see p72).

4 Amelia Earhart Park
A fun and wholesome day out. There's a petting zoo with lots of baby animals and pony rides on weekends. There are also

Parrots, Metrozoo

islands to search out, beaches to explore, playgrounds, and fish-filled lakes. Blacksmiths demonstrate their skills, as do other craftsmen, and the whole is delightfully uncrowded, as the park is well away from the tourist track. ◎ 401 E 65th St, at NW 42nd Ave • 305-685-8389 • 9am–4:30pm daily • Adm

5 Miami Metrozoo
This zoo is an endless delight for children. At the children's petting zoo, there are regularly scheduled "Ecology Theater" presentations, where children can touch all sorts of exotic species and learn about the local Florida environment as well. Also near the entrance is Dr. Wilde's World, where, among other hands-on exhibits, you can explore "The Wonders of Tropical America."

Hobie Beach

Other experiences include sniff stations, animal puzzles, and a sensory game wall (see p107).

6 Storytelling

Every Thursday at 7pm, in the plush, beautiful lobby of the historic Biltmore Hotel in Coral Gables, it's storytelling time around the fireplace. Youngsters may also enjoy a visit to the inches in their elaborate cages, as well as a stroll around the gardens and the fountains within the grounds (see p99).

7 Historical Museum of Southern Florida

The Downtown museum has created a number of hands-on activities and multimedia programs, such as an exploration of the Everglades' ecology, past and present (see also p42).

8 Museum of Science and Planetarium

The young and curious will find much to capture their attention and imagination in this multi-faceted facility. There are over 140 hands-on exhibits to explore the worlds of sound, light, and gravity, not to mention the chance to hug a dinosaur. Outside – beyond the collections of fossils, mounted insects, spiders, and butterflies – lies the Wildlife Center, home to birds, tortoises, and enormous snakes. The state-of-the-art Planetarium offers laser light shows set to rock music. ⦿ 3280 S Miami Ave • Museum: 305-646-4200 • Planetarium: 305-646-4400 • www.miamisci.org • 10am–6pm daily; closed Thanksgiving & Christmas • Adm

9 Mini Amore – European Fashions for Children

If your kids are demanding designer duds, this is the top shop. Couturier masters such as

Miami Seaquarium

Moschino and Versace have begun creating trendy threads for the preschool-to-adolescent market. ⦿ 3015 Grand Ave, No. 173 CocoWalk, Coconut Grove • 305-444-8440 • Sun–Thu, 11am–10pm, Fri & Sat, 11am–midnight

10 Key West Aquarium

The Touch Tank is a great attraction for children, allowing them to pick up starfish, native conchs, and horseshoe crabs. Elsewhere, they even get the chance to pet a live shark. When it opened, in 1934, this was Key West's first tourist attraction, and it continues to draw capacity crowds, not only for its hands-on features, but also for the highly entertaining and educational guided tours. Seeing the amazing and rare sawfish go to work during feeding time is not to be missed. ⦿ 1 Whitehead St at Mallory Square • Map A6 • 305-296-2051 • www.keywestaquarium.com • 10am–6pm daily • Adm

AROUND MIAMI AND THE KEYS

Miami Beach and
Key Biscayne
70–81

Downtown and
Little Havana
82–89

North of Downtown
90–97

Coral Gables and
Coconut Grove
98–105

South of
Coconut Grove
106–113

The Keys
114–125

Side Trips
126–131

MIAMI'S TOP 10

Left **Art Deco hotel** Center left **Jet skier** Right **Mynt Nightclub**

Miami Beach and Key Biscayne

NOWHERE ELSE ON EARTH *seems to be so happily addicted to glamour as Miami Beach. All the traits of modern life are here, pushed to the limit: symbols of speed, wealth, and status are vaunted everywhere you look in this body-conscious, sexually charged resort. Key Biscayne, the next big island to the south, provides a stark contast to the dynamism and self-consciousness of its neighbor; here you will find a tranquil and family-oriented atmosphere pervading parks, perfect beaches, and a scattering of museums.*

Delano Hotel

Map labels:
- Bass Museum of Art
- DADE BOULEVARD
- Miami Beach
- Watson Island
- Parrot Jungle Island
- Wolfsonian Museum
- SoBe & Deco District
- MACARTHUR CAUSEWAY
- Lummus Island
- Government Cut
- Biscayne Bay
- Fisher Island
- Virginia Key
- RICKENBACKER CAUSEWAY
- Atlantic Ocean
- Miami Seaquarium
- Marjory Stoneman Douglas Biscayne Nature Center
- Crandon Park
- Biscayne Bay
- CRANDON BOULEVARD
- Key Biscayne
- Harbor Drive
- Key Biscayne
- Atlantic Ocean
- Bill Baggs Cape Florida State Park
- Cape Florida Lighthouse
- 1 ⌐ miles ⌐ 0 ⌐ km ⌐ 1

10 Sights

1. SoBe and the Deco District
2. Parrot Jungle Island
3. The Wolfsonian
4. Bass Museum of Art
5. Miami Seaquarium
6. Crandon Park
7. Marjory Stoneman Douglas Biscayne Nature Center
8. Harbor Drive
9. Bill Baggs Cape Florida State Park
10. Cape Florida Lighthouse

Park Central Hotel

Cavalier Hotel, Deco District

1 SoBe and the Deco District

Posh high-life and decadent low-life meet and the fun never stops in the vibrant beach-and-nightclub community of South Beach – otherwise known as SoBe (see pp8–9). The world-famous Deco District (see pp10–13), an essential element of Miami Beach, is beautifully preserved in hundreds of colorful, inspired buildings.

2 Parrot Jungle Island

See more than 3,000 species of animals and over 110 species of plants at this 18.6-acre theme park. The centerpiece is the beautiful tropical gardens, and a highlight is the park's world-famous bird show, with parrots, storks, macaws, cockatoos, cranes, a Blythe hornbill, and other unusual birds. But there are more than birds here: there is a huge collection of reptiles (including a rare albino alligator) and poisonous snakes, in the serpentarium, and

a petting farm with lots of friendly animals. You don't even have to pay admission to enjoy the beautiful views at the Lakeside Cafe – it overlooks a sea of pink flamingos in Flamingo Lake. ⊛ Watson Island in Biscayne Bay nr the Port of Miami • www.parrotjungle.com • 305-400-7000 • 10am–6pm • Adm

3 The Wolfsonian

A wonderful museum and design research institute that traces the origins of Deco and other significant modern artistic trends within this 1920s' former storage facility (see pp22–3).

The Wolfsonian façade

4 Bass Museum of Art

This Mayan-influenced Deco structure of the 1930s came of age in 1964, when John and Johanna Bass donated their extensive collection of art. It consists mainly of 15th–17th-century European paintings, sculpture, and textiles, and highlights include Renaissance and Baroque works, as well as paintings by Rubens, and a 16th-century Flemish tapestry. ⊛ 2121 Park Ave, South Beach • Map S1 • 305-673-7530 • www.bass museum.org • 10am–5pm Tue–Sat (open to 9pm Thu); 11am–5pm Sun; Adm (free admission 2nd Thu of every month

Ghirlandaio painting, Bass Museum

Killer whale, Miami Seaquarium

enormously wide, with palm trees and picnic areas. The waters are calm and shallow, and good for snorkeling. There are also concession stands, 75 barbecue grills, a winding boardwalk, and convenient parking. ✎ Map H3
• 305-361-6767

5 Miami Seaquarium

This has been a Miami institution since the 1960s, when the hit TV series *Flipper* was filmed here. Trained dolphins still swim in the cove where Flipper once swam, and you can join them under a trainer's watchful eye for a fee. There are live shows throughout the day, featuring sea lions and killer whales as well as dolphins. Other areas provide viewing stations to see manatees, sharks, a mangrove of pelicans, and a coral reef aquarium. ✎ 4400 Rickenbacker Causeway, Virginia Key
• Map H3 • 305-361-5705 • www.miami seaquarium.com • 9.30am–6pm daily; Adm

6 Crandon Park

Key Biscayne is blessed with some of Miami's top beaches. Certainly the most impressive is this one, which is actually rated among the top ten in the country. Located on the upper half of the key, it's 3 miles (5 km) long and

Miami Vice

September 16, 1984, was a day that was to transform Miami almost overnight. It was the day *Miami Vice* debuted on TV, setting the stage for this city to conquer the world of high-profile glitz and hedonism. Suddenly the slick, cotton-candy-colored world of edgy outlaws, fast cars, and deals caught the global imagination, and Miami was the place to be.

7 Marjory Stoneman Douglas Biscayne Nature Center

Part of Crandon Park, this center contains a unique black mangrove reef of fossilized wood and roots along the northeast shore of Key Biscayne. Wearing suitable foot protection, you can wade in shallow waters to explore the underwater world. The nature center is named after the woman who almost single-handedly saved the Everglades from being overrun by housing developments, and it offers information and guided tours. ✎ 4000 Crandon Blvd, Key Biscayne • Map H4

8 Harbor Drive

Winding along the western shore, this is the heart of Key Biscayne's upscale residential district. The lucky ones with houses on the outer side of the road have magnificent views of Downtown Miami from their back gardens. Although the area has its share of mansions, most of the houses are more modestly proportioned. Still, it's a rarefied neighborhood where flocks of ibis can be found picking away on someone's lawn. ✎ Map G4

9 Bill Baggs Cape Florida State Park

This beach, also rated among the nation's top ten, is conveniently joined to picnic areas and

Boardwalk, Bill Baggs

pavilions by boardwalks across the dunes. The sugary sand is sometimes marred by clumps of seaweed, but it is the stinging man-o'-war jellyfish that you need to watch out for most.
◎ Map H4 • 305-361-5811 • Adm

10 Cape Florida Lighthouse
The oldest structure in South Florida has been standing sentinel since 1825. In 1836, it was destroyed by Native Americans, only to be reborn 10 years later. It has since withstood some blistering meteorological onslaughts, but the worst threat came from simple neglect following its dismissal from duties 1878. Only in 1966 did its renovation and preservation begin. ◎ Map H4 • Tours at 10am and 1pm; 109 steps to the top

Cape Florida Lighthouse

A Walk Through the Deco District

Morning

🕐 From the southern end of the District on **Ocean Drive**, at 6th Street, head northward, checking out not just the façades but also as many of the hotel interiors as you can. Many have unique design elements in the lobbies, bars, and gardens.

Between the **Leslie** and the **Cardozo** is the wonderful **Carlyle**, currently undergoing a major restoration.

Turn left after the Cavalier, and go to the next next street over, **Collins Avenue**. Turn right on Collins and check out **Jerry's Famous Deli** at 1450, built in curved Nautical style in 1939 by Henry Hohauser. Stop here for lunch.

Mid-afternoon

A little farther on, you'll find the **St. Moritz Hotel**, which features a cut coral façade and neon.

At 1685, you can't miss the all-white **Delano**, with its landmark winged tower. The outlandish post-modern interiors are by Philippe Starke, and contain original Dali and Gaudi furniture.

Next stop is the **Ritz Plaza**, with another fantasy tower in glass block. When you get to 21st St, turn left; on the next corner you will encounter the **Abbey Hotel**, with its marvelous salamander motif and Flash Gordon-style towers.

🔵 Head back to Collins Ave, and at 1775 you'll find **The Raleigh Hotel** – it's a beautiful location for drinks.

For more on the Deco District **See pp10–13**

Left **Fishing** Center **Cycling** Right **Diving**

TOP 10 Sports Options

1 Swimming
The hotel pool or the surging gray-blue Atlantic Ocean? This is Florida, and swimming is number one – snorkeling, too, in quieter areas, especially Crandon Park on Key Biscayne (see p72) and off South Pointe.

2 Volleyball
Anywhere there's a developed beach, you'll find a volleyball net and a quorum of players. Lummus Park is the best place to show off your skills to Miami's greatest beach bums, but South Pointe Park's a close contender.

3 Fishing
Deep-sea fishing out in the ocean, or the more conventional kind off a jetty or pier – both are readily available. The jetty or Sunshine Pier at First Street Beach on Miami Beach is good, or the breaker area just south of the Lighthouse on Key Biscayne.

4 Bicycling
The best way to get around both Miami Beach and Key Biscayne. ◎ Mangrove Cycles, 260 Crandon Blvd, Key Biscayne, 305-361-5555 • Miami Beach Bicycle Center, 601 5th Street, South Beach, 305-674-0150.

5 Jet-skiing
At Hobie Island Beach (see p30) you can rent one of these exciting modes of fun on the water, or head over to Virgina Key and you'll find Jet Ski Beach, with lots of rental stands.

6 Tennis
There are plenty of tennis courts all over the islands. ◎ Information about public courts, Miami-Dade County Parks and Recreation Department, 305-755-7800 • Flamingo Tennis Center, 1000 12th St, S Beach

7 Golf
So that he could play golf year-round is the main reason that Jackie Gleason (see p39) moved to Miami. The Crandon Golf Course is one of the best. ◎ 6700 Crandon Boulevard, on Key Biscayne • 305-361-9129.

8 Windsurfing and Surfing
For windsurfing, the intra-coastal waterways are calmer and there's almost always a breeze; check out Windsurfer Beach on Virginia Key for rentals. For surfing, the waves on the Atlantic side are plenty gnarly; the best spot is just off First Street Beach.

9 Kite-Flying
A very popular activity, given the prevailing maritime winds. There's even a park especially for kite enthusiasts at the south end of Haulover Park.

10 Workouts
South Pointe Park has a "Vita Course," a fitness circuit you can huff and puff your way through while taking in the view of the port, and enjoying the relative spaciousness compared to the crowds of Lummus Park.

Left **SoBe shops** Right **Morgan on Collins Avenue**

TOP 10 Shopping

1 Collins Avenue at 7th Street, South Beach

The block or two around this intersection has all the designer boutiques you'll ever need, from Versace Jeans Couture to Club Monaco, with its carefully select-ed knockoffs. Also check out the side-street stores. ◈ *Map R4*

2 Soho Clothing, Miami Beach

A huge selection of jeans for men, women, and kids, as well as shirts and unusual jewelry. ◈ *645 Lincoln Road • Map R2*

3 Public House, South Beach

Here the stars are the cigars, imported from everywhere but Cuba. Newspapers are also available. ◈ *1059 Collins Ave, South Beach • Map S4*

4 Art Deco District Welcome Center

A treasure-trove of Deco kitsch to take home as your very own. Everything from cutesy salt-&-pepper sets to really rather nice reproduction lamps. ◈ *1001 Ocean Drive, South Beach • Map S4*

5 Anthropologie, Miami Beach

Chic couture. Complete ensembles from loungewear to skirts and jackets. Also full lines of accessories, including shoes, handbags, and jewelry. Located in Lincoln Road Mall. ◈ *1108 Lincoln Road • Map Q2*

6 Kafka's Used Book Store & Cyber Café

Yes, books in the middle of South Beach, and a reference to Franz Kafka, no less. Just in case you suddenly start feeling intellectual on the beach. ◈ *1464 Washington Ave, at 14th St, South Beach • Map S3*

7 Books and Books, Miami Beach

Find the perfect read while working on your tan. Also has a café serving Pan-American food. ◈ *933 Lincoln Road • Map R2*

8 Fritz's Skate Shop

Get yourself a pair of in-line skates, to rent or buy, and take some free lessons (Sunday mornings). Surf boards available, too. ◈ *730 Lincoln Road • Map R2*

9 Heart and Soul, Miami Beach

An eclectic and funky store selling contemporary jewelry for men and women, as well as watches and other unique gift items. A great range of accessories for the home and office. ◈ *411 Espanola Way • Map R2*

10 Key Biscayne

The Square Shopping Center, 260 Crandon Boulevard, and several other generic types nearby are just about all that you'll find on Key Biscayne. They contain a few art galleries, small clothing boutiques, and the usual mix of banks, chain stores, and dentists. ◈ *Map H4*

Miami Beach also has markets on Española Way and Lincoln Road – See p57

Left **Score** Right **Twist**

TOP 10 Gay and Lesbian Venues

1 Twist
SoBe's largest gay venue has recently expanded, and there's something on every night of the week. Happy hour daily 1–9pm. ✆ *1057 Washington Ave, South Beach • Map R4 • 305-538-9478 • www.twistsobe.com • 1pm–5am daily*

2 Creme Lounge
This recently redesigned club has a "Siren" lesbian night on Saturdays, Latin music on Tuesdays, "Creme & Sugar" fun night on Thursdays, and a hip-hop party on Fridays. ✆ *725 Lincoln Lane, South Beach • Map R2 • 305-535-1163*

3 Laundry Bar
It's not all about suds at this much-frequented laundromat and full-service bar, alive with clean, cruisy locals and a throbbing dance beat. ✆ *721 Lincoln Lane at Meridian Ave • Map R2 • 305-531-7700*

4 Buck 15 Lounge
An intimate New York-style lounge. Thursday nights are particularly hot, attracting a fun, young, and fashionable crowd. ✆ *707 Lincoln Lane, South Beach • Map R2 • 305-538-3815*

5 Madiba
This elegant restaurant and lounge (formerly known as Jade) has a happy hour, two resident DJs, and various special events. Don't miss the popular "Euphoria" drag show on Friday nights at 11pm. ✆ *1766 Bay Rd, South Beach • Map Q2 • 305-695-1566*

6 Score
SoBe's best mix of all-gay bar and dance club. It pairs a big-room interior with sidewalk-café style. Located right on Lincoln Road in the heart of South Beach. ✆ *727 Lincoln Rd, South Beach • Map R2 • 305-535-1111*

7 Balans
This London import is a firm favorite in the gay community. Offering a global menu (including their signature lobster club sandwich) with a dash of British style *(see p79)*. ✆ *1022 Lincoln Rd, Miami Beach • 305-534-9191 • 8am–midnight (to 1am Fri and Sat nights)*

8 Palace Bar and Grill
Formerly called Studio. Comfort food, artists' sanctuary, and bar, at the epicenter of gay life at the beach. ✆ *12th & Ocean, South Beach • Map S3 • 305-531-7234*

9 Coliseum
This gay night spot is very popular and full of beautiful creatures dancing to some of the top DJs in the city. Located near Fort Lauderdale's Hollywood airport, but worth the trip out there. ✆ *2520 S Miami Rd • 954-832-0100 • www.coliseumnightclub.com*

10 Boy Bar
This new addition to the nightclub scene attracts a mixed crowd who enjoy its relaxed and friendly atmosphere. Outdoor barbecue on Sundays. ✆ *1220, Normandy Dr, Miami Beach • Map H2*

For gay and lesbian venues in other parts of South Florida See pp52–3

Left **crobar** Center **Mynt** Right **Opium Garden**

Nightlife

1 Jazid
As the name would suggest, a more low-key choice, where you can listen to jazz and blues by candlelight, and, presumably, feed your id. ✆ *1342 Washington Ave, South Beach • Map R3 • 305-673-9372*

2 crobar
Housed in the former Cameo movie theater, this place employs high-tech prestidigitations to give you the sense of floating in a Surrealist's dreamworld. ✆ *1445 Washington Ave, South Beach • Map S3 • 305-531- 8225 • www.crobarmiami.com*

3 Penrod's Complex
A good-value club, with several bars and dance floors. Downstairs is the upbeat Nikki Beach, with a non-stop party atmosphere. Upstairs is the exclusive Pearl Lounge. ✆ *1 Ocean Dr, South Beach • Map R5 • 305-538-1111*

4 Bongos Cuban Café
This hot nightclub, started by Gloria Estefan, usually has some in-house professional dancers on the floor to get the crowd dancing. Latin food, such as chicken, pork, and fried bananas, is also served. ✆ *601 Biscayne Blvd • Map P1 • 786-777-2100*

5 Opium Garden
Favored by the likes of Julia Roberts, this open-air venue is one of the most exclusive, so be prepared to wait. Mostly house music. ✆ *136 Collins Ave, at 1st St, South Beach • Map R5 • 305-531-5535*

6 Mynt
Go – even if it's just to sample a tipple or two from the cocktail menu. This stylish, sophisticated nightspot is for a hip South Beach crowd. ✆ *1921 Collins Ave, Miami Beach • Map S2 • 786-276-6132*

7 Mansion
Originally built as a movie theater, this Art Deco space is one of the hottest clubs in South Beach. It has four rooms: hip-hop, house, progressive, and a VIP area. ✆ *1235 Washington Ave, Miami Beach • Map R3 • 305-531-5535*

8 Tantra Restaurant and Lounge
Tantra pleases all the senses, with the stunning interior – fresh-grass floor, water wall, fiber optic "sky", and erotic art. Enjoy the food, aphrodisiac drinks, and new-age music. ✆ *1445 Pennsylvania Ave, Miami Beach • Map R3 • 305-672-4765*

9 B.E.D.
Don't be a couch potato, go to B.E.D. instead. A bubbling mix of gay and straight, and, yes, there are actual beds for lounging on. ✆ *929 Washington Ave, South Beach • Map R4 • 305-532-9070*

10 Blue
Very laid back and cool, as in the color that dominates in this fun cocktail bar-and-club. Musical nights include tropical house, flashbacks, flow, and soul. ✆ *222 Española Way, South Beach • Map S3 • 305-534-1009*

For more on Miami's famous nightlife See pp58–9

Left **Van Dyke Café** Right **Terrace at the Tides**

TOP 10 Sidewalk Cafés

1 News Café
Numero uno on Ocean Drive, it's spacious and bustling, perfect for a drink, snack, or meal, and avid people-watching *(see also p8)*. ⊗ *800 Ocean Drive, at 8th St • Map S4 • $*

2 Mango's Tropical Café
Always hot, with upbeat music and a huge Floribbean menu. The action spills outside. ⊗ *900 Ocean Drive, at 9th St • Map S4 • $$*

3 Clevelander
Facing the beach and on the sidewalk, there's always something going on here: listening to the live music, having something to eat, or just checking out the passersby. ⊗ *1020 Ocean Drive, South Beach • Map S4 • $*

4 Van Dyke
In the heart of Lincoln Road Mall, this is a prime spot for viewing the street parade. A good place for breakfast or lunch. Live jazz upstairs. ⊗ *846 Lincoln Rd, South Beach • Map R2 • $*

5 Starbucks
The Starbucks on Ocean Drive is predictably always busy. The outside tables are perfect for watching the world go by while enjoying a snack and a coffee. ⊗ *1451 Ocean Drive, South Beach • Map S3 • $*

6 Pelican Café
Grab a seat on the outdoor patio and indulge yourself, just as Cameron Diaz, Antonio Banderas, and Johnny Depp have before you, in gawking at the SoBe procession and partaking of the Mediterranean-style delectables. ⊗ *826 Ocean Drive, South Beach • Map S4 • $*

7 Front Porch Café
Many consider the breakfast here to be the best in South Beach. The atmosphere's homey, and the food's definitely worth the wait. ⊗ *Penguin Hotel, 1418 Ocean Drive, South Beach • Map S3 • $*

8 Larios on the Beach
Co-owned by pop Cuban songstress Gloria Estefan, it's *cocina cubana* prepared SoBe-style. Try the appetizer sampler for starters and some *rico mojitos* (yummy rum drink with mint leaves). ⊗ *820 Ocean Drive, South Beach • Map S4 • $*

9 Terrace at the Tides
Very chic outdoor dining. Sit where celebrities have sat and tuck into the gourmet cooking: maybe lobster gazpacho or coconut mascarpone cheesecake. ⊗ *1220 Ocean Drive, South Beach • Map S3 • $$*

10 Wet Willie's
This bar attracts a young, rowdy, post-beach crowd with its powerful frozen drinks with names such as Call Me a Cab. Nibbles to accompany the drinking include tasty fried calamari. ⊗ *760 Ocean Drive, South Beach • Map S4 • $*

Note: *Unless otherwise stated, all restaurants accept credit cards, have disabled access, and serve vegetarian meals*

Left **Mark's** Right **Tap Tap**

Restaurants

Price Categories

For a three-course meal for one with half a bottle of wine (or equivalent meal), taxes, and extra charges.	**$** under $20
	$$ $20–$40
	$$$ $40–$55
	$$$$ $55–$80
	$$$$$ over $80

1 Mark's South Beach
Master-chef Mark Militello offers a wonderful fusion dining experience. Culinary stunners may include tenderloin of beef with roasted garlic purée on a polenta crouton. Desserts are extraordinary, too, and the wine selection perfect *(see also p60)*. ✪ *Hotel Nash, 1120 Collins Ave, South Beach • Map S3 • 305-604-9050 • $$$$*

2 Tap Tap
Real Haitian food, some of it fiery with red chilies. Try the grilled conch with manioc or the shrimp in coconut sauce, with mango sorbet for dessert *(see also p60)*. ✪ *819 5th Street, South Beach • Map R5 • 305-672-2898 • $$*

3 11th Street Diner
Classic diner from 1948, originally built in Pennsylvania. ✪ *1065 Washington Ave, at 11th St, South Beach • Map R4 • 305-534-6373 • $$*

4 Joe's Stone Crab
Gloriously sweet stone crabs and a notorious wait to get in. Also fish – grilled, broiled, blackened, fried, or sautéed – pork, lamb, and steaks, and Miami's best Key lime pie *(see also p61)*. ✪ *11 Washington Ave, South Beach • Map R5 • 305-673-0365 • $$$*

5 Escopazzo
Solid Italian fare. Swordfish carpaccio, asparagus flan, and risotto are hits *(see also p60)*. ✪ *1311 Washington Ave, South Beach • Map S3 • 305-674-9450 • $$$$*

6 Pacific Time
Sample tasty experimental meldings of Pacific Rim and Caribbean. Tuna tartar with Idaho potato chips, Szechuan grilled Florida Keys grouper, and broiled Florida grapefruit are typical *(see also p60)*. ✪ *915 Lincoln Rd, South Beach • Map R2 • 305-534-5979 • $$$$*

7 China Grill
A fusion cuisine pioneer. Portions are not pretentiously miniscule; tastes are light and cleverly composed. Try the sake-marinated chicken. ✪ *404 Washington Ave, S Beach • 305-534-2211 • $$$$$*

8 Yuca
Young Urban Cuban-Americans. South Florida's original upscale Cuban restaurant. Nuevo Latino cuisine, live entertainment, and a trendy decor. ✪ *501 Lincoln Road, Miami Beach • Map R2 • 305-532-9822 • $$$$*

9 Barton G – The Restaurant
The lush, tropical orchid garden is a great setting for a romantic evening under the stars. Popular with locals, the food is neo-classic American. ✪ *1427 West Ave, Miami Beach • 305-672-8881 • $$$$*

10 Balans
An eclectic mix of Asian and Mediterranean influences, this chic, London-style café is popular, loud, and a SoBe standard-bearer. Great for a non-buffet Sunday brunch. ✪ *1022 Lincoln Road, South Beach • Map R2 • 305-534-9191 • $$$*

Following pages **Bright colors of an Art Deco-style beach patrol station on South Beach**

Left **Mosaic on dome of Gesu Church** Right **Bayside Marketplace**

Downtown and Little Havana

A LITTLE RUNDOWN, *this part of Miami is a foreign land for most Americans, but – if you are willing to make the cultural adjustment – it is a fascinating land. Here along the Miami River is where it all started in the late 1800s, but it took the arrival of Cuban exiles from the 1950s on for Miami to come into its own as a world player. On these brash streets, you will see that the influx from countries to the south has yet to abate and that the face of Miami is more Latino each day.*

🔟 Sights

1. Miami-Dade Cultural Center
2. Freedom Tower
3. US Federal Courthouse
4. Bayside Marketplace and Bayfront Park
5. Bank of America Tower
6. Gusman Center for the Performing Arts
7. Flagler Street
8. Gesu Church
9. Ingraham Building
10. Calle Ocho and Around

Tiles, Little Havana

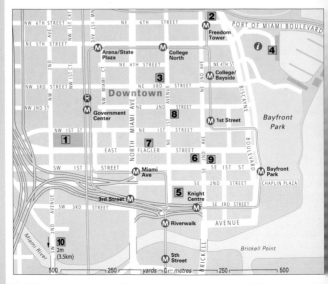

Miami-Dade Cultural Center

1 Miami-Dade Cultural Center

Designed by the celebrated American architect Philip Johnson in 1982, the Mediterranean-style complex, set around a tiled plaza, incorporates the Miami Art Museum *(see p42)*; the Historical Museum of Southern Florida *(see pp42–3)*; and the Main Public Library, which contains four million books. ◉ *101 West Flagler St, Downtown • Map M2 • Library 9am-6pm Mon–Sat (to 9pm Thu), 1–5pm Sun*

2 Freedom Tower

Downtown's landmark was built in 1925 in the Mediterranean-Revival style, inspired by the Giralda, an 800-year-old bell tower in Seville, Spain. Initially home to the now-defunct *Miami Daily News*, its role and name changed in the 1960s, when it became the reception center to process more than 500,000 Cubans fleeing Castro. It was restored in 1988 to create a Cuban museum, which is located in the lobby of the building. ◉ *600 Biscayne Blvd, Downtown • Map N1*

3 US Federal Courthouse

This imposing Neo-Classical edifice, finished in 1931, has hosted a number of high-profile trials, including that of Manuel Noriega, the former Panamanian president, in 1990. The spartan jail cell where he awaited trial on international drug-trafficking charges is also in this building. The main attraction is the second-floor mural entitled *Law Guides Florida's Progress*, designed by Denman Fink, famous for his work in Coral Gables. It depicts Florida's evolution from a tropical backwater to one of America's most prosperous states. ◉ *301 North Miami Ave, Downtown • Map N1 • 8am–5pm Mon–Fri, closed public hols & during major trials*

4 Bayside Marketplace and Bayfront Park

Curving around Miamarina, this shopping and entertainment complex is undeniably fun and the Downtown area's best attraction. It's not South Beach, but La Vida Loca echoes here, too, often with live salsa bands playing on the esplanade. Shops – including Guess?, Victoria's Secret, Structure, and Foot Locker – and 30 eateries, with everything from ice cream to paella, make it a happening place. To the south, Bayfront Park, designed by Isamu Noguchi, is extensive and can provide a pleasant interlude of greenery, water, monuments, sculpture, and striking views. ◉ *401 Biscayne Blvd at 4th St, Downtown • Map P1–2 • www.baysidemarketplace.com • 10am-10pm Mon–Thu, 10am–11pm Fri & Sat, 11am–9pm Sun*

Freedom Tower

Left **Bank of America Tower** Right **Ingraham Building**

5 Bank of America Tower

The city's most striking sky-scraper is the work of architect I. M. Pei, perhaps most famous for putting the glass pyramid in the courtyard of the Louvre in Paris. This building is notable both during the day for its Op-Art horizontal banding across the stepped hemi-cylinders, and at night for the changing, sophisticated colors of its overall illumination. Built in 1983, the office building was known first as Centrust Tower, but it now bears the moniker of its current principal tenant. ◈ *International Place, 100 SE 1st St., Downtown • Map N2*

6 Gusman Center for the Performing Arts

Built in 1926, this theater has a fabulously ornate Moorish interior and is housed in the similarly colorful and festooned Olympia Building. It began as a vaudeville theater, where Rudy Vallee used to perform, and Elvis Presley also gigged here. Inside, the hall looks like an Arabian Nights palace, with turrets, towers, intricate columns, and a crescent moon and stars in the ceiling. Buy a ticket to anything just to see it. ◈ *174 E Flagler St, at SE 1st Ave., Downtown • Map N2 • Box Office 305-372-0925*

Gusman Center

Gateway to Latin America

Two-thirds of Miami's population is of Hispanic origin. Pick up the *Miami Herald* and you'll see that the news of the day in Caracas, Bogotá, Managua, and above all Havana is given top billing. All these connections, for good or ill, have made Miami the US kingpin in dealing with Latin and South America.

7 Flagler Street

Flagler is Downtown Miami's main drag – loud, bright, busy, and lined with small shops and street peddlers. Pop into the Galería International Mall (243 East Flagler Street, at SE 2nd Avenue) for cheap and tasty ethnic snacks, while on the next block is the stylish Gusman Center. On East Flagler Street at NE 2nd Avenue, look for the Alfred I. DuPont Building (1937–9), a paean to Art Deco in the Depression Moderne style. ◈ *Map N2*

8 Gesu Church

This Mediterranean-Revival building in the Spanish Colonial style (built 1922) is the oldest Catholic church in Miami. Dozens of masses are held every week, in English and Spanish. The church is noted for its stained-glass

Gesu Church

windows, which were made in Munich, Germany. The ceiling mural was restored in its entirety by a lone Nicaraguan refugee in the late 1980s. ✆ *118 NE 2nd St, Downtown • Map N1 • 305-379-1424*

9 Ingraham Building

Completed in 1926, this is a kind of Neo-Renaissance work: the building's twelve stories are clad in Indiana limestone and its roof sheathed in Spanish tiles. The interior is opulent, featuring a lavish ceiling decorated in gold leaf, with the building's insignia cast in brass. The lobby's light fixtures, the mailbox, and the office directory are all original. Picked out in gold on the elevator are scenes of South Florida wildlife. ✆ *25 SE 2nd Ave, at E. Flagler St, Downtown • Map N2*

10 Calle Ocho and Around

A slice of Cuban culture, liberally spiced up with all sorts of other Hispanic and Caribbean influences. Since Castro's Communist revolution in Cuba, Miami has become ever more Cubanized by wave after wave of immigrants from the embattled island they still long for as home *see pp14–15*).

A Trip Through Calle Ocho

Mid-morning

🕐 First stop, if you like a cigar, is **El Crédito** *(see pp14 & 88)* on SW 11th Ave. Just a few doors along you'll find the **Botánica El Aguila Vidente** *(see p88)*. Let your eye wander over the shop's plethora of paraphernalia, most of all the colorful plaster statues.

Next stop is at SW 13th Avenue, to pay your respects to fallen Cuban freedom fighters at the **Brigade 2506 Memorial Eternal Flame** *(see p14)*, before a sortie into the delightful fruit market at 1334, **Los Pinareños Fruteria** *(see p88)*.

At the corner of SW 15th Ave, peek in on **Domino Park** *(see p15)* where there's always at least one game going on. And now comes time to stop for coffee and maybe a snack at the wonderful **Exquisito** *(see p89)*. Try to grab one of the vibrantly colored tables outside.

Late morning

Continuing on to the next block, at 1652, take in the exciting Latin American art at the **Agustín Gaínza Gallery** *(see p88)*, where you're likely to meet the affable artist himself.

After that, try a free-form ramble of discovery – but don't miss the gaudy entrance to **La Casa de los Trucos** *(see p88)*, at 1343 – and when it's time for lunch, head for **La Carreta I** *(see p89)*, on the south side of Calle Ocho. Enjoy good Cuban food at reasonable prices.

Around Miami – Downtown and Little Havana

*The Top 10 sights of Little Havana are covered on **pp14–15***

Left **Latino theater, Calle Ocho** Right **Metromover**

TOP 10 Walks, Drives, and Viewpoints

1 Bayside Marketplace
Adjacent to the impressive American Airlines Arena, this complex feels part Disney theme-park, part international bazaar. Right on the waterfront, it's always good for a stroll *(see p83)*.

2 Flagler Street
Walking through the heart of Downtown Miami is reminiscent of a marketplace you might encounter in Latin America – colorful, brash, rather seedy – and none too safe at night *(see p84)*.

3 Calle Ocho Walk
The area between 11th and 17th Avenues is excellent for walking. You can check out ethnic shops and sample various Cuban delicacies along the way *(see p85)*.

4 Architectural Walk
The buildings highlighted on pages 83–5 are lined up over about six blocks along NE–SE 1st and 2nd avenues. Another building worth a look is the Neo-Classical-Revival Miami-Dade County Courthouse, three blocks away. Don't miss the ceiling mosaics in the impressive lobby. ◈ *Map N1–2*

5 A Drive through Little Havana
To get the overall feel and extent of Little Havana, it's best to drive, from José Martí Park in the west to about 34th Avenue in the east, where the Woodlawn Cemetery and Versailles Restaurant are located *(see p15)*.

6 Views of Downtown
Some of the best views of Downtown are afforded from the freeways. Coming across MacArthur Causeway from South Beach, you'll get some dazzling perspectives, especially at night. The finest view of the skyline is from the Rickenbacker Causeway. ◈ *Maps P1 & M6*

7 A Ride on the Metromover
The Metromover consists of two elevated loops around Downtown, so it's a great way to get an overview of the area *(see p137)*.

8 A Calle Ocho Café
The Exquisito Cafetería *(see p89)* is the best on the street and a wonderful place to listen to the music and watch the fascinating street life all around.

9 A Stroll in José Martí Park
This charming little park by the Miami River is graced with colonnades and pavilions, Spanish-style clusters of street lamps, palm trees, and an excellent children's playground. ◈ *Map M2*

10 A Stroll in Bayfront Park
Right on beautiful Biscayne Bay, Noguchi designed this park "as a wedge of art in the heart of the New World." Here, in addition to Noguchi's sculptures you will find lush greenery, a small sand beach, tropical rock garden, cascading fountain, palms and olive trees. ◈ *Map P1–2*

Left **Los Ranchos of Bayside** Right **Gusman Center**

Lively Latino Arts Venues

1 Teatro de Bellas Artes
This Calle Ocho venue presents eight Spanish plays and musicals a year. Most of the plays are Spanish originals, but there are also plays in translation, such as Tennessee Williams' *A Streetcar Named Desire*. ✪ 2173 SW 8th St • 305-325-0515

2 Porcão
This Brazilian supper club and bar features some of the best live Brazilian music in town, especially when sultry singer Rose Max performs: Thur and Fri Happy Hours. ✪ *Four Ambassadors Hotel, 801 Brickell Bay Dr • 305-373-2777*

3 Cultura del Lobo
The Performance Series presents music, dance, film, and visual arts, with an emphasis on contemporary works and solo theater performers. ✪ *Miami-Dade Community College, Wolfson Campus 300 NE 2nd Ave, at NE 3rd St*

4 Teatro Ocho
Home to the Hispanic Theater Guild, which regularly presents Spanish-language theater. Its directors try to choose topical plays that will stir public opinion and become a force for renewal in the Cuban community. ✪ 2101 SW 8th St

5 Venevision
Latin stage productions, including comedy, make this popular with locals. ✪ 1560 S. Dixie Highway • 305-663-5410

6 Casa Juancho
This popular restaurant is loacted in Little Havana and serves up award-winning cuisine, as well as excellent Spanish performances. Besides the piano bar and strolling guitarists, there is a fine flamenco show. ✪ 2436 SW 8th Ave, Little Havana • 305-642-2452

7 Manuel Artime Theater
A former Baptist church, this Downtown facility has been converted into an 800-seat state-of-the-art theater and is the home of the Miami Hispanic Ballet, which produces the annual International Ballet Festival. ✪ 900 SW First St • 305-575-5057

8 Gusman Center for the Performing Arts
The major Downtown venue *(see p84)* often features Latin American performances of all types, including films during the annual Miami Film Festival.

9 Los Ranchos of Bayside
Located in Bayside marketplace, this popular and casual restaurant features Latin cuisine as well as American steakhouse fare. Latin entertainment also provided. ✪ 401 Biscayne Blvd • 305-375-8188

10 Casa Panza
Great flamenco performances several nights a week at this authentic Spanish restaurant right in the Cuban heart of Calle Ocho *(see p89)*.

Miami's more mainstream arts venues are on **pp38–9**

Left **Botánica El Aguila Vidente** Center **Agustin Gaínza Gallery** Right **Los Pinareños Fruteria**

TOP10 Cuban/Latino Shopping

1 Botánica El Aguila Vidente
The most atmospheric and mysterious of the botánicas along the main section of Calle Ocho *(see pp15 & 48)*.

2 Agustín Gaínza Gallery
The gallery's namesake, a celebrated Cuban artist, shows his works here, as well as those of other contemporary Cuban and Latin American artists. ✎ *1652 SW 8th St • Map J3 • 305-644-5855*

3 Old Cuba, The Collection
This welcoming little store specializes in Cuban art, music, books, and clothing, as well as dominoes, coffee-makers, and fine cigars. The owner, Jackie Perez, also promotes a mini-street-festival of the arts held on the last Friday of each month. ✎ *1602 SW 8th St • Map L3 • 305-643-6269*

4 El Crédito
A raggedy old factory, where you can watch cigars being rolled and breathe in the sweet perfume of pure tobacco *(see p14)*.

5 Los Pinareños Fruteria
A delightful fruit market for finding all sorts of exotic Caribbean produce, such as mamey and small "apple" bananas. There's also a wonderful café and fresh juice bar. ✎ *1334 SW 8th St • Map K3*

6 La Casa de los Trucos
If you're in town for Carnaval or Halloween, this is the place to come for all your costuming needs. From the most predictable to the most bizarre, this shop has a vast inventory and excellent prices, to buy or rent. ✎ *1343 SW 8th St • Map K3 • 305-858-5029*

7 Havana Shirt
Get the best in Cuban shirts, as well as touristy beach shirts, from this store which has a huge range. It is located in the trendy Bayside Marketplace shopping center. ✎ *401 Biscayne Blvd • Map K3 • 305-373-7720*

8 Havana To Go
If you are interested in Cuban memorabilia, this store is bound to have it. Items on sale include reproductions of Cuban artwork, telephone books and, of course, cigars. ✎ *1442 SW 8th St • Map J3 • 305-857-9720*

9 Emme Brazilian Sportswear
This sexy Brazilian sportswear can be found at Gold's Gym on Miami Beach. The light, dry-fit material looks great and it does not wrinkle so it is easy to pack. ✎ *Gold's Gym 1400 Alton Road, South Beach • Map G3 • 305-535-2214*

10 Casino Records
There are at least seven record shops between 11th and 17th streets, each with outside speakers, keeping the street energy on high. Cubans live for music, and Casino provides Latin sounds in abundance. ✎ *1208 SW 8th St • Map K3 • 305-856-6888*

Price Categories

For a three-course	**$** under $20
meal for one with half	**$$** $20–$40
a bottle of wine (or	**$$$** $40–$55
equivalent meal), taxes,	**$$$$** $55–$80
and extra charges.	**$$$$$** over $80

Left **Versailles** Right **El Atlakat**

🔟 Cuban/Latino Food

1 Versailles

A Little Havana institution, Versailles is actually a Cuban diner in a very sleek guise *(see pp15 & 60)*. ◈ *3555 SW 8th St, at SW 35th Ave • Map G3 • 305-444-0240 • $$$*

2 Garcia's Seafood Grille & Fish Market

A family-run eatery with a friendly atmosphere, in- and outdoors, though you might have a bit of a wait. Great grouper chowder, and conch salad. ◈ *398 NW North River Dr • Map L1 • 305-375-0765 • $$*

3 Exquisito Restaurant

The most authentic and affordable on the street, where locals go every day. All the gritty Cuban fare, like brain fritters and horse beef stew, but also Cajun lobster or shrimp and pork chops for the "gringos". ◈ *1510 SW 8th Street (Calle Ocho), Little Havana • Map J3 • 305 643-0227 • $$$*

4 El Atlakat

The cuisine of El Salvador, served in a spacious, cheerful setting. Pleasant murals, and a menu that leans toward chicken and seafood. ◈ *3199 SW 8th St • Map G3 • 305-649-8000 • $$$*

5 La Carreta I

From the food to the clientele, this family restaurant is thoroughly Cuban. Located in the heart of Little Havana, good food at reasonable prices ensures its popularity. Open late. ◈ *3632 SW 8th St • Map G3 • 305-444-7501 • $$$*

6 Casa Panza

A picturesque Spanish restaurant, known for its fine paella and authentic flamenco show. Rooms are cozy, with different flamenco performers several nights of the week. ◈ *1620 SW 8th St • Map J3 • 305-643-5343 • $$$*

7 Old Lisbon

A taste of Portuguese cuisine, with *sardinhas assadas* (grilled sardines), *salada polvo* (octopus salad), mussels, squid, and assorted cheeses. ◈ *1698 SW 22nd St • Map J5 • 305-854-0039 • $$$$*

8 El Crucero

Old-fashioned hospitality, Cuban style, and amazing cooking. Daily specials are listed on the board. Don't miss the creamy *natilla*, a sweet custard with a caramelized top, which rounds off a meal perfectly. ◈ *7050 SW 8th St • Map F3 • 305-262-1966 • $$*

9 Cancun Grill

Mexican food at its best. Try the fish ceviche, the *taquitos rancheros*, and the plantain nachos. ◈ *15406 NW 77th Court, Miami Lakes • Map G2 • 305-826-8571 • $$$*

10 Guayacan

Cozy and unpretentious, this is Cuban fare with a zingy Nicaraguan twist. Try the *pescado a la Tipitapa*, a whole red snapper deep-fried and drenched in a sauce of onions and peppers. Wonderful soups, too. ◈ *1933 SW 8th St • Map J3 • 305-649-2015 • $$$*

> **Note:** Unless otherwise stated, all restaurants accept credit cards, have disabled access, and serve vegetarian meals

Left **Bal Harbour boutique** Center **Design District** Right **Gulfstream Park Race Track**

North of Downtown

THE AREAS NORTH of Miami Beach and Downtown are an irreconcilable juxtaposition of urban
sprawl and urban chic, of downtrodden ethnic and
high-flying elite. Little is actually scenic, although
the beaches are among the area's greatest. Indeed,
much of northern Miami has the reputation of a slum. There's local color
to be discovered, but the vibes can
be less than welcoming, and you
should be careful. Still, some of
Greater Miami's most scintillating
sights, including one of the oldest
buildings in the Americas, and fine
dining can also be found here.

Downtown fashion

Sights

1 Ancient Spanish Monastery
2 Little Haiti
3 Opa-Locka
4 Gulfstream Park
5 Bal Harbour
6 Museum of Contemporary Art
7 Design District
8 Haulover Park and Beach
9 Arch Creek Park and Museum
10 Greynolds Park

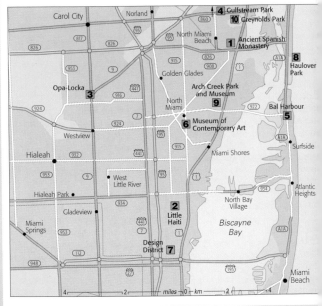

Take extra care when visiting Opa-Locka and Little Haiti, and
when driving through Hialeah. Avoid Liberty City and Overtown.

Left **Iron ornamentation, Ancient Spanish Monastery** Right **Façade in Little Haiti**

1 Ancient Spanish Monastery

This is the oldest European-tradition building in the Western Hemisphere, originally built in 1133–41 near Segovia, Spain. In 1925, William Randolph Hearst bought the magnificent cloisters, had them dismantled stone by stone, and sent to the US. After many trials and tribulations, the stones were reassembled here in the early 1950s for $1.5 million. Call before visiting on weekends as the monastery will close for events such as weddings. *(See page 93.)* ® *16711 W Dixie Hwy, North Miami Beach • Map H1 • 305-945-1461 • www. spanishmonastery.com • 10am–5pm Mon–Sat, 1:30–5pm Sun • Adm*

2 Little Haiti

Little Haiti is not so much dangerous as disconcerting – to see so much poverty just steps away from such wealth. The one attempt at promoting tourism was the Caribbean Marketplace. Though critically acclaimed, it has had mixed success. ® *NE 2nd Ave, from about NE 55th to NE 80th • Map G2 • Marketplace at 5927 NE 2nd Ave*

3 Opa-Locka

Nicknamed the "Baghdad of Dade County," the fantasy follies of this now-depressed district were the brainchild of Glenn Curtiss in the 1920s. All in pink, with minarets, burnished domes, and keyhole arches, the restored City Hall is the best example left. (But don't stray far from it.) ® *Cnr NW 27th Ave & NW 135th St • Map G2*

4 Gulfstream Park

Thoroughbreds race here on two tracks between January and April, and the park is also home of the prestigious million-dollar Florida Derby, which takes place in March every year. During the racing season, concerts are held here on weekends, with national and international performers. ® *901 S Federal Hwy, Hallandale • Map H1 • 954-454-7000 • www.gulfstreampark.com*

City Hall, Opa-Locka

For personal security tips **See p139**

Haulover Beach Park, north of Bal Harbour

5 Bal Harbour

The Barrier islands north of Miami Beach are occupied mainly by posh residential areas, and this is the poshest. Known for its flashy hotels and one of the swankiest malls anywhere, Bal Harbour is said to have more millionaires per capita than any other city in the US. Bal Harbour Shops – note the British spelling – is a determinedly snooty place in a tropical setting, whose tone is set by the wealthy grandes dames and the security staff in neo-colonial uniforms and pith helmets. Elsewhere along 96th Street, you'll find galleries, gourmet shops, and a swarm of plastic surgery studios. ◉ Map H2

6 Museum of Contemporary Art

The museum (MOCA) opened its state-of-the-art building to the public in 1996. It's known for its provocative exhibitions and for

Museum of Contemporary Art

Class and Culture Clash

Greater Miami is a bubbling cauldron of cultural diversity. Many endemically underprivileged African-American communities lie within a stone's throw of exclusive shops. In other areas, impoverished recent immigrants – from Cuba, Haiti, and other Central American countries – eke out miserable existences in huddled quarters of endless urban blight.

seeking a fresh approach in examining the art of our time. ◉ 770 NE 125th St • Map G2 • 305-893-6211 • www. mocanomi.org • 11am–5pm Tue–Sat, noon–5pm Sun • Adm • Tours on Sat at 2pm

7 Design District

It started out as a pineapple grove, but from the 1920s this zone was being called Decorators' Row because of the design stores that had moved in. For a while in the '80s, due to high crime, the area fell on hard times, but things are picking up again, and top-end design, furniture, and fixture shops once again rule. Photographers and artists have been moving here, too, to escape the high rents of South Beach. ◉ Nr Buena Vista between NE 36th–41st Sts and from NE 2nd to N Miami Aves • Map G2

Design District

8 Haulover Park and Beach

Haulover Park contains one of south Florida's most beautiful beaches – a mile and a half of golden sand drawing people from all walks of life. Nestled between the Intercoastal Waterway and the Atlantic, the beach is ideal for surfing and swimming and on warm weekends it is jam-packed with sun bathers. The park itself has a marina, restaurant, tennis courts, a nine-hole golf course, and a kite shop. ✆ *10800 Collins Ave • Map H1 • 305-947-3525*

9 Arch Creek Park and Museum

Created around a natural limestone bridge formation, this location used to be part of an important Native American trail. A museum/nature center contains artifacts left by those peoples. Naturalists will be your guides as they point out native birds, animals, insects, and trees. ✆ *1855 NE 135 St • Map G2*

10 Greynolds Park

An oak-shaded haven for runners, golfers, and other outdoor enthusiasts, Greynolds Park is landscaped with native and exotic plants, including mangrove, royal palm, palmetto, pampas grass, sea grape, and gumbo limbo. You'll also find beach volleyball courts, a children's playground, and plenty of picnic tables. ✆ *17530 W Dixie Hwy • Map H1 • Adm weekends*

A Tour of the Ancient Spanish Monastery

Morning

Drive north from central Miami on Highway 1 (also called Biscayne Blvd). The road is lined with shops – stop off at any that catch your eye. Turn left on NE 163rd St, then right onto W Dixie Hwy (also NE 22nd Ave). The **Ancient Spanish Monastery** *(see also p91)* is on the right after the canal.

You may well feel a sense of awe as you walk around this beautiful little piece of medieval Europe on US soil. Even European visitors, who have visited many such buildings in their homeland, might still marvel at the dedication of Hearst to put it here.

For the best route through the grounds, start at the gift shop/museum, exit to the patio, through the gardens, cloisters, interior rooms, culminating with the chapel, and back through the gift shop.

Among the notable sights are an 800-year-old birdbath, a life-size statue of the Spanish king Alphonso VII (the monastery was constructed to commemorate one of his victories over the Moors), and two of only three known surviving round stained-glass windows from the 12th century.

Afternoon

In keeping with the Spanish-inspired theme, eat at nearby **Paquito's Mexican Restaurant** *(see p95)* and take a detour along NE 2nd Ave through colorful **Little Haiti** *(see p91)* on your way back.

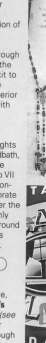

Left **Vierge Miracle lotions and potions store** Right **Collectibles at Divine Trash**

Unusual Shops

1 Vierge Miracle & Botànica Saint Philippe
Right in the heart of Little Haiti, it doesn't get more authentic than this. It's helpful if you can speak French to find out more about the soaps, sprays, and lotions. ◈ 5910 NE 2nd Ave • Map G3

2 Minar
Oriental rugs – some very old and exquisite – art, textiles, wall-hangings, and ceramics from Central Asia and China. The atmosphere is delightfully Eastern, right down to the tea served. ◈ 6667 Biscayne Blvd • Map G3

3 Divine Trash
All sorts of antiques, art, collectibles, and various found objects. The upbeat, charming proprietor, Donna Ashby, is something of a local celebrity. Don't miss her orchid garden and the great day spa upstairs (see no.4). ◈ 7244 Biscayne Blvd • Map G3

4 Addict
Fashion sneakers for all the family. Here you will find a wide selection of rare sneakers not widely available in department stores. ◈ Bal Harbour Shops, 9700 Collins Ave • Map H2 • 305-864-1099

5 Art By God
Impressive mineral/nature store, with dinosaur fossils, natural and carved semiprecious gemstones, insects, shells, butterflies, skulls, animal mounts, etc. ◈ 3705 Biscayne Blvd • Map G3

6 Intermix
Outfits for the discerning woman, whether 18 or 50. A great range of prices, labels, and accessories. ◈ Bal Harbour Shops, 9700 Collins Ave • Map H2 • 305-993-1232

7 It's A Take
Everything needed for a romantic dinner: place settings, linens, decorative objects galore, gourmet treats, and a florist. ◈ 6924 Biscayne Blvd • Map G3

8 Mini Oxygene
The place to buy brand-name clothes for children, from Armani to Mona Lisa. ◈ Bal Harbour Shops, 9700 Collins Ave • Map H2 • 305-868-4499

9 Diable En Deuil Botánica
If you want luck or for your lover to behave, there are ways… and this is the place to find them: Haitian powders, potions, and iconographic figures abound, some of them very sexually graphic. ◈ 8009 NE 2nd Ave • Map G3

10 The Art of Shaving
A complete range of men's grooming products. You can also get a haircut. ◈ Bal Harbour Shops, 9700 Collins Ave • Map H2 • 305-865-0408

The Art of Shaving

Price Categories

For a three-course meal for one with half a bottle of wine (or equivalent meal), taxes, and extra charges.

$	under $20
$$	$20–$40
$$$	$40–$55
$$$$	$55–$80
$$$$$	over $80

La Paloma

10 Places to Eat

1 Soyka
Run by the same fellow as the News Café *(see p8)*, this is a huge, bistro-like setting with an adventurous Italianesque fusion menu. The sesame-seared salmon with spinach, shiitakes, and sweet soy sauce is not only alliterative but also sensationally scrumptious. ◎ 5556 NE 4th Ct • Map G3 • 305-759-3117 • $$$

2 P. F. Chang's China Bistro
This bright, modern restaurant has an open kitchen, serving family-style Chinese food. Try the wok-seared lamb or the prawns with green pearls. ◎ 17455 Biscayne Blvd • Map G3 • 305-957-1966 • $$$

3 Andiamo!
A jaunty little place that specializes in brick-oven pizza, choice panini, salads, and tasty desserts like the homemade cannoli. ◎ 5600 Biscayne Blvd • Map G3 • 305-762-5751 • $$

4 Bice
Outstanding Milanese-inspired cuisine. The friendly staff serve generous portions. ◎ 18683 Collins Ave, Sunny Isles Beach • Map H2 • 305-503-6011 • $$$$

5 Hanna Gourmet Diner
Homemade soups; inventive salads, such as tomato with fennel and goat cheese; snapper française; steak au poivre; and an unforgettable fruit tart. ◎ 13951 Biscayne Blvd • Map G3 • 305-947-2255 • $$$

6 Chef Allen's
International fusion artistry at its finest. The Indian-influenced dishes include "cowboy" steak with tamarind and chili and lobster-crab cakes with chutney. Hazelnut "Kit-Kat" bars make an unusual finish. ◎ 19088 NE 29th Ave • Map G3 • 305-935-2900 • $$$$$

7 La Paloma
Old-World ornate, borderline kitsch décor. A superb house salad comes with every entrée. Try oysters Rockefeller or veal Milanese. ◎ 10999 Biscayne Blvd • Map G3 • 305-891-0505 • $$$$$

8 Paquito's Mexican Restaurant
Expect fresh tortilla soup, steak Paquitos sautéed in a jalapeño and onion sauce, and a yummy *mole verde*. ◎ 16265 Biscayne Blvd • Map G3 • 305-947-5027 • $$$

9 Wolfie Cohen's Rascal House
There is always a line at this no-reservations restaurant, but for good reason. The menu features favorites such as cabbage rolls and pot roast. Open from 6:30am daily until late. ◎ 172nd and Collins Ave • Map H2 • 305-947-4581 • $$$

10 The Crab House Seafood Restaurant
All types of seafood, such as snow crab legs and oysters. Try the all-you-can-eat cold seafood bar. ◎ 1551 NE 79th St Causeway • Map G3 • 305-868-7085 • $$$

Note: Unless otherwise stated, all restaurants have disabled access, accept credit cards, and serve vegetarian meals

Left **Venetian Pool** Center **One of Merrick's fantasies** Right **Lowe Art Museum**

Coral Gables and Coconut Grove

CORAL GABLES AND COCONUT GROVE, *taken together, constitute one of the most upscale neighborhoods in Greater Miami. The former is actually a separate city, while the latter is a district of Miami, its oldest, and the site of the Miami City Hall. Coral Gables was one of the nation's first "planned" cities and is consistently posh from end to end. Coconut Grove is a more variegated mosaic, historically the focus of Miami's intellectual, bohemian community but also incorporating the blighted "Black Grove", where the descendants of Bahamian workers often live in real squalor.*

🔟 Sights

1. Biltmore Hotel
2. Venetian Pool
3. International Villages
4. Miracle Mile
5. Lowe Art Museum
6. CocoWalk
7. Villa Vizcaya
8. Barnacle Historic State Park
9. Peacock Park
10. Dinner Key

Exhibit, Midori Gallery

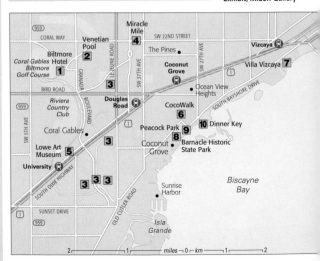

Biltmore Hotel

1 Biltmore Hotel

George Merrick was one of the visionaries who made Florida into what it is; this lavish hotel stands as a monument to his taste and grand ideas. Herculean pillars line the grand lobby, and from the terrace you can survey the largest hotel swimming pool in the country. Johnny Weismuller, the first movie Tarzan, used to teach swimming here, and the likes of Al Capone, Judy Garland, and the Duke and Duchess of Windsor came in its heyday. Weekly tours of the hotel and grounds depart from the front desk *(see also pp18 & 146)*. ◈ Map F3

2 Venetian Pool

One of the loveliest and most evocative of Merrick's additions to his exotic vision for Coral Gables. The pool is fed by springs and was the site of at least one movie starring Esther Williams, the 1940s water-ballet beauty *(see also p18–19 & 64)*. ◈ Map G3

3 International Villages

Merrick's architectural flights of fancy still add a special grace note to beautiful, upscale Coral Gables. All are private homes, but you can drive by and take in their unique charms *(see also pp18–19)*. ◈ Map G4

4 Miracle Mile

In 1940, a developer hyped the town's main shopping street by naming it Miracle Mile (a mile if you walk up one side and down the other). Colorful canopies adorn shops as prim and proper as their clientele. Buildings of note are Merrick's Colonnade Building, at No. 169, with its splendid rotunda, huge ballroom, Spanish fountain, and Corinthian columns; and, on nearby Salzedo Street at Aragon Avenue, the Old Police and Fire Station, 1939, with square-jawed sculpted firemen. ◈ *Coral Way between Douglas and Le Jeune • Map F–G3*

5 Lowe Art Museum

Greater Miami's finest art museum boasts solid collections of ancient and modern world art *(see pp20–21)*. ◈ Map F3

Left **Façade, International Villages** Right **Colonnade Building, Miracle Mile**

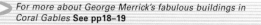

For more about George Merrick's fabulous buildings in Coral Gables See pp18–19

99

Left **CocoWalk mall** Right **Villa Vizcaya**

CocoWalk
6 This compact, two-story center is the heart of Coconut Grove Village, and features some good shopping, dining, and entertainment. The atmosphere is, in fact, that of a village. People are hanging out, zipping by on in-line skates and bikes, checking each other out. Often live music is happening right in the middle of it all. The main attraction in the evening is probably the multiplex cinema. ◈ *3015 Grand Avenue* • *Map G3* • *www.cocowalk.com*

Villa Vizcaya
7 One of the most historic and beautiful places in the Greater Miami area; this icon of the city's cultural life is not to be missed *(see pp16–17)*. ◈ *Map G3*

Barnacle Historic State Park
8 Hidden from the highway by a tropical hardwood hammock (mound), this is Dade County's

Barnacle Historic State Park

Grand Plans in the Grove and Gables
The area called Coconut Grove was the first in the Miami area to be settled. Following the Civil War, in 1868, Edmund Beasley responded to the Homestead Act of 1862, claiming his 160 acres of land here, his free if he could only manage to live on it for five years and make some improvements, which he did. It took the genius of George Merrick, some 60 years later, to dream the notion of preplanning an entire ideal city – Coral Gables *(see pp18–19)*.

---

oldest home. It was designed and built in 1891 by Commodore Ralph Munroe, who made his living as a boat builder and a wrecker (salvager). In fact, wood from shipwrecks was used to build the house, and it was inventively laid out to allow the circulation of air, all-important in those days before air-conditioning. Rooms are stuffed with old family heirlooms, old tools, and wonderful early appliances. ◈ *3485 Main Highway, Coconut Grove* • *Map G3* • *305-442-6866* • *www.floridastateparks.org* • *9am–4pm Fri, Sat, Sun, Mon; by reservation Tue, Wed, Thu* • *Closed national holidays* • *1-hour tours at 10 & 11:30am, 1 & 2:30pm* • *Adm*

9 Peacock Park

In the 1960s, this was where the Grove hippies grooved, and on weekends now and when there's a festival, some of the old magic gets temporarily resurrected. The park is named after Charles and Isabella Peacock, who built the area's first hotel, the Peacock Inn, which at the time was the only hotel between Palm Beach and Key West. The park is now largely a baseball field, and there's also a rustic Chamber of Commerce building. ® *2820 MacFarlane Ave, at Bayshore Drive, Coconut Grove • Map G3*

10 Dinner Key

The name derives from the early days when settlers had picnics here. In the 1930s, Pan American Airways transformed Dinner Key into the busiest seaplane base in the US. It was also the departure point for Amelia Earhart's doomed round-the-world flight in 1937. The airline's sleek Streamline Moderne terminal houses the Miami City Hall, and the hangars are now mostly boatyards, though one is the famous Monty's Stone Crab Seafood House and Raw Bar *(see p105)*. The marina here is now the most prestigious in Miami, so walk along and enjoy inspecting the yachts berthed here. ® *5 Bayshore Drive, Coconut Grove • Map G3*

Dinner Key

A Tour of Coconut Grove Village

Morning

🕐 This walk is designed for Friday–Monday, because it begins with a tour of the **Barnacle Historic State Park**. Try to get there for the 10am tour, and notice the distinctive roof, which gives the house its name.

As you exit, turn left and go down to the corner of Devon Road to enjoy the Mission-style **Plymouth Congregational Church** *(see p47)*, built in 1916. If they're open, pop into the back gardens.

Now walk back along Main Highway several blocks to 3500, the **Coconut Grove Playhouse** *(see p38)*, a handsome Mediterranean-Revival building that dominates the corner at Charles Avenue. Continue along Main Highway to the next street, then stop for lunch and some top-notch people-watching at the every-busy **Green Street Café** *(p102)*.

Afternoon

After lunch, walk up Commodore Plaza to visit 3168, the **Midori Gallery** *(p104)*. Afterwards, continue on to Grand Avenue and turn right; go down a couple of blocks to the major intersection and cross the street into the shopping mecca **CocoWalk**.

On the next block, Rice Street, look up to admire the fanciful façade of **The Streets of Mayfair** mall *(p104)*. To finish off your tour, visit nearby **Johnny Rockets** *(p102)* for a snack in this 1950s diner located in the center of all the excitement.

Left **CocoWalk entrance** Right **Johnny Rockets**

TOP 10 Special Places and Events

1 Books and Books
One of Greater Miami's best bookstores, set amid graceful arcades (see p104).

2 CocoWalk
A compact shopping and entertainment center right in the heart of Coco Village – always something or someone to catch the eye (see p100).

3 Johnny Rockets
This 1950s-style diner opposite CocoWalk is always jumping. Order a burger and fries and watch the whole of the Grove go by sooner or later. ◊ *3036 Grand, cnr of Main Hwy, Coconut Grove*

4 Green Street Café
Almost always crowded, this corner venue is another prime people-watching spot in the Grove. Sit and sip a drink or order up a full meal. ◊ *3110 Commodore Plaza, Coconut Grove • 305-444-0244*

5 King Mango Strut
An outrageous local tradition that sends up the year's events and celebrities, harking back to the days when the Grove was a haven for intellectuals and eccentrics. The party climaxes with a concert and dance in Peacock Park. ◊ *Last week of December • Starts at Main Hwy & Commodore Plaza, Coconut Grove*

6 Coconut Grove Arts Festival
Perhaps Greater Miami's best such festival, attracting throngs of visitors who come to eat, drink, listen to concerts in Peacock Park, and browse among 300 arts and crafts booths. ◊ *Three days over the third weekend in Feb • Throughout the Grove, especially Bayshore and Peacock Parks • www.coconutgroveartsfest.com*

7 Miami-Bahamas Goombay Festival
A Bahamian party that includes a parade, Island food, Caribbean music, and *junkanoo* dancers parading through the streets. It claims to be the biggest African-American heritage festival in the US. ◊ *First weekend in Jun • Throughout the Grove*

8 Miami International Orchid Show
Florida has become one of the world centers for the orchid industry. More than half a million blooms are displayed at this show. ◊ *Early Mar • Coconut Grove Convention Center, 2700 S. Bayshore Drive, at SW 27th Ave • 305-255-3656*

9 The Improv Comedy Club
Enjoy some of the country's best stand-up comics, have a delicious dinner, or even take a lesson on how to be a comic. ◊ *3390 Mary Street, Shoppes of Mayfair, Coconut Grove • 305-441-8200*

10 Columbus Day Regatta
Some 600 boats take part. ◊ *Mid-Oct • Coral Reef Yacht Club to Elliot Key • www.columbusdayregatta.net*

Left **Chinese Village, designed by Merrick** Right **Coral Gables Merrick House**

🔟 Walks, Drives, and Historic Sites

1 Miracle Mile
Though not really quite a mile, nor particularly miraculous, this street and parallel ones are mostly about nice shops and elegant eateries *(see p99)*.

2 Coconut Grove Village
This is a place to walk *(see p101)*, but it's probably best not to venture more than a few blocks west of CocoWalk ("Black Grove," sadly, is uninviting). ◐ *Map G3*

3 Merrick Villages
Driving around Coral Gables to take in these charming residences, done up in the styles of various national and regional cultures, will take perhaps a couple of hours *(see pp18–19)*.

4 Barnacle Historic State Park
This unusual house, lived in by the descendants of its original builder until 1973, is the area's oldest, built in 1891 *(see p100)*.

5 Villa Vizcaya
A recreation of a 16th-century Italian villa with formal gardens *(see pp16–17)*.

Vizcaya grotto

6 Biltmore Hotel
Inimitably beautiful and grand, this is one of the world's most gorgeous hotels, opened in 1926 *(see p99)*.

7 Congregational Church
Merrick's deliciously Baroque paean to his father, a Congregational minister, was Coral Gables' first church and remains the city's most beautiful *(see p19)*.

8 Venetian Pool
Considered the world's most beautiful public swimming pool. You could spend half a day enjoying its charms *(see pp18 & 99)*.

9 Coral Gables Merrick House
The boyhood home of George Merrick *(see p19)* has been restored to its 1920s look, and it's remarkable to reflect on how modest the man's background was compared to the grandeur of the dreams he realized. The city of Coral Gables took its name from this house. The stone was quarried from what is now the Venetian Pool. ◐ *907 Coral Way • 305-460-5361 • House 1–4pm Wed & Sun; grounds, 8am–sunset daily • Adm*

10 Coconut Grove Playhouse
In a reversal of the usual story, this period Mediterranean-Revival building, in the Spanish Rococo style, was built in 1926 as a movie house and later converted to a theater *(see p38)*.

Left **Midori Gallery** Right **Books and Books**

🔟 Boutiques

1 Modernism Gallery
One of the country's top dealers in ultracool furniture, lighting fixtures, and accessories, including Art Deco. ✪ *800 Douglas Road, Suite 101, Coral Gables • by appt*

2 Midori Gallery
Exquisite, museum-quality Chinese and Japanese ceramics, lacquers and ivories, some as old as the Eastern Han Dynasty, 25–220 AD. Other sublime pieces from the Sung Dynasty, about 1,000 years ago. ✪ *3168 Commodore Plaza, Coconut Grove*

3 Palm Produce Resortwear
Florida lifestyle clothing means loose and colorful, natural fabrics, and somewhat frivolous designs for both men and women. ✪ *3390 Mary Street, Streets of Mayfair, Coconut Grove • Map G3*

4 The Gilded Hand
This store carries hand-crafted gifts and fashionable accessories for the body and home. There's also fine art, curios, antiques, and unusual silver and gold jewelry. ✪ *165 Aragon Ave, Coral Gables • Map G3*

5 Book and Books
Just a block off the Miracle Mile is this wonderful bookshop specializing in arts and literature, and books on Florida. There's a great café, frequent poetry readings, and book signings. Upstairs you'll find a rare books room and photo gallery. ✪ *265 Aragon Ave, Coral Gables • Map G3*

6 White House
A rarified range of women's fashion, all of it white. Elegant, sequined evening gowns, smart suits, peignoirs, and underthings. Prices suit the quality of the fabrics and workmanship.
✪ *3015 Grand Ave, CocoWalk • Map G3*

7 Expertees Golf Shop
With all the very latest lines of clubs and putters, and accessories, this shop also offers a state-of-the-art computerized swing analysis, shaft lab, club fitting center, and lessons for beginners and low handicappers.
✪ *2329 Coral Way • Map G3*

8 Hibiscus Hill
A unique gift shop with a captivating range of handmade objects: elaborate jewelry, hand-blown glass, and imported *objets*, all with a distinctly fabulous air. And mostly fabulous prices, too. ✪ *Streets of Mayfair, 2911 Grand Ave, Coconut Grove • Map G3*

9 Out of Africa
The sound of African drums fills the air, and hand-carved wooden figures and masks, and silver jewelry fill the space. ✪ *Streets of Mayfair, 2911 Grand Ave, Coconut Grove • Map G3*

🔟 Barnes & Noble Booksellers
Not just a complete bookstore, but also a snack and coffee bar, and a great place to hang out. ✪ *152 Miracle Mile, Coral Gables • Map G3*

Price Categories

For a three-course meal for one with half a bottle of wine (or equivalent meal), taxes, and extra charges.	**$** under $20
	$$ $20–$40
	$$$ $40–$55
	$$$$ $55–$80
	$$$$$ over $80

Left **Norman's** Right **The Cheesecake Factory**

TOP 10 Trendy Restaurants

1 Norman's
Norman Van Aiken is the country's chief protagonist of New World fusion cuisine. Experience opulent aspects of tuna, foie gras, fish, seafood, and even simple salad greens that you never knew existed. § 21 Almeria Ave, Coral Gables • 305-446-6767 • $$$$$

2 Restaurant Place St. Michel
A romantic spot, capturing the feel of Paris. Every bite is a thrill to the palate, although it is hardly French, with Caribbean-style dishes such as grilled fish with plantains and salsa. § Hotel Place St. Michel, 162 Alcazar Ave, Coral Gables • Map G3 • 305-446-6572 • $$$$

3 Christy's
Still packing them in after 20 years, this local favorite has been made a landmark by politicians, CEOs, and celebrities. Aged steak, fresh seafood, and award-winning caesar salad. § 3101 Ponce de Leon Blvd, Coral Gables • 305-446-1400 • $$$$

4 Monty's Stone Crab Seafood House and Raw Bar
A vast dining room in an old airplane hangar. Try the Jamaican jerk spiced fish, or the excellent peel-and-eat shrimp and raw oysters. It's a Miami insititution. § 2550 S Bayshore Drive, Coconut Grove • Map G3 • 305-858-1431 • $$$$

5 Giralda Café
The 1,000-year-old traditions of Peruvian cookery – e.g. fried yucca with *huancaina* sauce, fish and shrimp ceviche, and beef stew in cilantro (coriander) sauce. § 254 Giralda Ave, Coral Gables • Map G3 • 305-448-6064 • $$

6 Baleen
Fresh oysters shucked at your table, the best lobster bisque on Biscayne Bay, oak-smoked diver scallops, and Asian bouillabaisse are some of the treats. § 4 Grove Isle Drive, Coconut Grove • Map G3 • 305-857-5007 • $$$$$

7 The Cheesecake Factory
One of six in South Florida, serving everything from pot stickers to shepherd's pie, and at least 36 types of cheesecake. § 3015 Grand Ave, CocoWalk • Map G3 • 305-447-9898 • $$$

8 Anokha Fine Indian Cuisine
Tandoori a specialty, and side dishes featuring homemade paneer cheese. § 3195 Commodore Plaza, Coconut Grove • 786-552-1030 • $$$

9 Titanic Brewing Company
Lift a pint of homemade brew and sample crawfish or calamari snacks. § 5813 Ponce de Leon Blvd, Coral Gables • 305-667-2537 • $$

10 Café Tu Tu Tango
"Food for the starving artist" is their by-line, and, indeed, artists and their works are all over the place. Wonderful light fare, such as seared sashimi tuna salad, and crispy shrimp brochettes. § CocoWalk • Map G3 • 305-529-2222 • $$

> **Note:** Unless otherwise stated, all restaurants have disabled access, accept credit cards, and serve vegetarian meals

Left **Charles Deering Estate** Right **Coral Castle**

South of Coconut Grove

HEADING SOUTH FROM MIAMI'S MAIN EVENTS, *once you get past the dull, nondescript suburbs, you enter vast tracts of citrus groves and tropical nurseries. The general mood changes, too – a bit backwoodsy, a bit Old South. Though sometimes gruff, the people here are friendly enough, and there are plenty of shopping opportunities, parks, gardens, zoos, and museums. You'll notice that the natural landscape looks a bit mauled – the area took the full brunt of Hurricane Andrew's muscle in 1992 and is still recovering.*

Left **Coral Castle sculpture** Right **Fairchild Tropical Garden**

🔟 Sights

1. **Fairchild Tropical Garden**
2. **Charles Deering Estate**
3. **Miami Metrozoo**
4. **Monkey Jungle**
5. **Coral Castle**
6. **Wings Over Miami**
7. **Gold Coast Railroad Museum**
8. **Biscayne National Underwater Park**
9. **Florida International University Art Museum**
10. **Fruit & Spice Park**

1 Fairchild Tropical Garden

This dizzyingly beautiful tropical paradise was established in 1938 and serves also as a botanical research institute. Around a series of man-made lakes stands one of the largest collections of palm trees in the world (550 of the 2,500 known species), as well as countless other wonderful trees and plants. During a 40-minute tram tour, guides describe how plants are used in the manufacture of everything from Chanel No. 5 to golf balls. Allow another two hours to explore your own. ◊ 10901 Old Cutler Rd • Map G4 • 305-667-1651 • www.fairchildgarden.org • 9:30am–4:30pm daily • Adm

Miami Metrozoo

2 Charles Deering Estate

Right on Biscayne Bay, the estate contains two significant architectural works: Richmond Cottage, built in 1896 as the area's first inn, and a large Mediterranean-Revival "Stone House," built in 1922. You can also visit what is thought to be a Pre-Columbian burial site and a fossil pit. ◊ 16701 SW 72nd Ave, at SW 167th St & Old Cutler Rd • Map F4 • 305-235-1668 • 10am–4pm daily • Adm

3 Miami Metrozoo

The zoo works a great deal with endangered species. Zookeepers give talks at feeding times. ◊ 12400 SW 152 St • Map E4 • 305-251-0400 • www.miamimetrozoo.com • Adm

4 Monkey Jungle

This endearing attraction is still run by the family that founded it in 1933 to study the behavior of primates. Many of the smaller monkeys roam wild while you walk through caged walkways; the gorillas, orangutans, spider monkeys, and gibbons are kept in conventional cages. There are regular demonstrations of the capabilities of macaques, chimpanzees, and other human cousins. ◊ 14805 SW 216th St, Cutler Ridge • Map F5 • 305-235-1611 • www.monkeyjungle.com • 9:30am–5pm • Adm

5 Coral Castle

A castle it isn't, but a conundrum it certainly is. From 1920 to 1940, Latvian immigrant Edward Leedskalnin built this mysterious pile as a Valentine to the girl back home, who had jilted him in 1913. No one knows how he single-handedly quarried and transported the 1,100 tons of tough coral rock, carved all the enormous chunks into monumental shapes, and set them all into place so flawlessly. One nine-ton gate is so exquisitely balanced that it opens with the pressure of your little finger. ◊ 28655 South Dixie Hwy • Map E6 • 305-248-6345 • www.coralcastle.com • 9am–6pm Mon–Thu, 9am–9pm Fri–Sun • Adm

For a suggested day's itinerary incorporating the Deering Estate **See p109**

Coral Castle

6 Wings Over Miami

This military and classic aircraft museum acts as a tribute to early inventors, veterans, and aviators, some of whom set world records with the planes on display here. Exhibits include early biplanes and an all-plywood DeHavilland. ◈ *Tamiami Airport, 14710 SW 128th St at SW 147th Ave, South Dade • Map E4 • 305-233-5197 • www.wingsovermiami.com • 10am–5:30pm Thu–Sun • Adm*

7 Gold Coast Railroad Museum

The museum was started in 1957, by a group of Miamians who were trying to save threatened pieces of Florida history. Some of the earliest items in the collection are the "Ferdinand Magellan," a private railroad car built for President Franklin Roosevelt; the FEC engine that pulled a rescue train out from Marathon after the 1935 hurricane; and the 113 locomotive built in 1913. The Edwin Link is a small-gauge children's railroad. ◈ *12450 SW 152nd St • Map F4 • 888-608-7246 • www.goldcoast-railroad.org • 10am–4pm Mon–Fri, 11am–4pm Sat–Sun • Adm*

8 Biscayne National Underwater Park

Biscayne National Underwater Park is 95 percent water, therefore most visitors enter it

Hurricane Country

One in ten of the North Atlantic hurricanes hits Florida, which means an average of one big storm every two years. On August 24, 1992, Hurricane Andrew was one such storm, measuring 4 on the Saffir-Simpson Scale. The worst is a 5, like the one that hit the Keys in 1935, destroying the Flagler bridge.

by private boat. Otherwise, the Dante Fascell Visitor Center at Convoy Point is the only place in the national park you can drive to and, from there, you have several boating options. The concession offers canoe rentals, glass-bottom boat tours, snorkel trips, scuba trips, and transportation to the island for campers. There's also a picturesque boardwalk that takes you along the shoreline out to the rock jetty beside the boat channel heading to the bay. ◈ *SW 328th St (North Canal Drive) • Map D5 • 305-230-7275 • www.nps.gov/bisc • 8:30am–5pm daily*

Gold Coast Railroad Museum

9 Florida International University Art Museum

Dubuffet exhibit, University Museum

The museum specializes in Latin American and 20th-century American art and presents six to eight major exhibitions each year. The Martin Z. Margulies Sculpture Park displays 69 works in a variety of media distributed throughout the 26.5 acres of the FIU campus – a wonderfully rich and important representation of modern work. It is recognized nationally as one of the world's great collections of sculpture and the largest on a university campus. It includes major pieces by Dubuffet, Miro, Nevelson, Calder, Noguchi, and Serra. ⊗ *University Park, PC 110 • Map F3 • 305-348-2890 • 10am–9pm Mon, 10am–5pm Tue–Fri, noon–4pm Sat & Sun • 1-hr tours throughout year • Free*

10 Fruit & Spice Park

This 30-acre (12-ha) tropical botanical park is devoted to exotic plants, such as citrus fruits, grapes, bananas, herbs, spices, nuts, and bamboo. It forms a unique attraction in the United States – after all, South Florida's tropical climate is found nowhere else in the US. The astonishing number of varieties on display include a selection of poisonous species and hundreds of bamboo and banana varieties. A wonderful store enables you to stock up your cupboards with many unusual fruit products. ⊗ *24801 Redland Road (SW 187th Ave), Homestead • Map E6 • 305-247-5727 • 10am–5pm daily • Adm/guided tours*

Deering Estate Walk

Morning

To get to the **Charles Deering Estate** *(see p107)*, drive south from Miami on Hwy 1 (also called the Dixie Hwy) and turn left on SW 168th St. Follow it until it deadends at the Estate on SW 72nd Ave.

A full tour of the grounds will take 3–4 hours. Follow the Entrance Trail to begin, and as you emerge from the mangroves you will encounter a splendid vista of Biscayne Bay. Note the water level marker, showing the inundation caused by Hurricane Andrew.

Richmond Cottage, the original structure here, was built as an inn in 1896. It was destroyed by Andrew in 1992, but has since been replicated. The elegant Stone House next door contains bronze and copper doors, portraits of the Deering family, a celebrated wine cellar, and more besides.

Head over to the Carriage House, where you can see a vintage gas pump. If you have time, take the Main Nature Trail, which crosses a handsome coral rock bridge, built in 1918. Finally, walk out through the historic Main Entrance, with its coral rock pillars and wood and iron gates.

Afternoon

Picnicking on the grounds is a possibility, and some facilities are provided. Or, for an elegant lunch, head south to the **Cauley Square Tea Room** *(see p111)*. To make a full day's outing, head farther south along Hwy 1 to the eccentric **Coral Castle** *(see p107)*.

Around Miami – South of Coconut Grove

Left **D'Ester** Right **Unicorn Creations**

Regional Souvenir Shops

1 Unicorn Creations
A fine range of antique, vintage, and exotic furniture from around the world, as well as home decor collectibles. ◈ Cauley Square, 22400 Old Dixie Highway • Map F5 • 305-258-1047

2 D'Ester
Home accessories of every description and a unique array of collectibles. ◈ Cauley Square, 12307 SW 224th St • Map F5 • 305-257-5535

3 Today's Collectibles
You'll have to step over the dogs as you enter from the front porch. Inside you'll find Tiffany-style lamps, marcasite and antique jewelry, furniture, and collectibles. ◈ Cauley Square, 12360 SW 224 St • Map F5

4 Cobblestone Antiques
Furniture, estate jewelry, early plates, and maps from pioneer days. ◈ 115 N Krome Ave, Homestead • Map E6 • 305-245-8831

5 Jay's Antiques and Collectibles
Baseball cards, coins, marbles, cookie jars, stamps, and comics. You can spend hours browsing here. ◈ 115 N Krome Ave, Homestead • Map E6 • 305-246-7060

6 The Aviary
Here's the place for you if you've finally decided you must sport a macaw or cockatoo on your shoulder. Plus, you can buy your new pet a Tiki Hut cage and all the seed and accoutrements it will need for a joyous, talkative life as your companion. A wonderful place to visit, laid out like a tropical garden. ◈ 22707 South Dixie Hwy • Map E5 • www.aviarybirdshop.com

7 Homestead Main Street
A pleasant little mall in downtown Homestead. Spaces, to the left as you enter, and Found Treasures, toward the end on the right, are very appealing. A classic shell-encrusted clock or mirror, for example, is utterly characteristic of regional Florida culture. ◈ 115 N Krome Ave, Homestead • Map E6 • 305-242-4814

8 Atabey
A fascinating range of unique arts and crafts and sculptures from around the world, including items and artifacts from Santa Domingo. ◈ Cauley Square, 22420 Old Dixie Highway • Map F5 • 305-257-5048

9 Island Colors
Paintings, sculptures, iron works, and souvenirs from Haiti and Africa. ◈ Cauley Square, 12309 SW 224th St • Map F5 • 305-258-2565

10 The Falls Shopping Center
One of the largest open-air shopping, dining, and entertainment complexes in the country. There are over 100 stores set in a waterscape with tropical foliage. ◈ US Highway 1 SW 136 St, South Miami • Map F4 • 305-255-4570 • www.shopthefalls.com

You'll recognize Cauley Square from Highway 1 as the quaint, Spanish-style hacienda off to the right as you head south

Left **Sushi** Right **Empanadas**

Regional Eateries

1 Red Fish Grill
One of Miami's most romantic spots, nestled amid the tropical magic of Matheson Hammock Park. Great, freshly caught fish, prepared lovingly with a Caribbean flair, and a range of other dishes. ◈ 9610 Old Cutler Rd • Map G4 • 305-668-8788 • $$$$

Sign for the Red Fish Grill

2 La Porteña
Traditional Argentine *parrillada*, but also thigs like ostrich, caviar crêpes stuffed with mascarpone and Manchego cheeses, and savory mussels sautéed with garlic. ◈ 8520 SW 8th St • Map F3 • 305-263-5808 • $$$$

3 Shula's Steak House
A beautifully appointed restaurant, with lots of Miami Dolphins memorablilia (it's owned by a former coach). As for the food, there is plenty of meat, including a giant 48 oz (1.35 kg) steak. ◈ 7601 Miami Lakes Dr, Miami Lakes • Map F2 • 305-820-8102 • $$$$

4 Tropical Chinese
Excellent Chinese food in a tropical, big, and busy setting. Expect abalone, shrimp with garlic and spinach in clay pots, and seafood tofu soup. ◈ 7991 Bird Rd • Map F3 • 305-262-7576 • $$$$

5 Trattoria Sole
The baby spinach salad with raisins and pinenuts works well, as does the polenta with wild boar sausage. ◈ 5894 Sunset Dr • Map F4 • 305-666-9392 • $$$$

6 Guadalajara
Original, home-cooked Mexican fare in a locale full of character. The portions are huge, so just an appetizer might do. Try dipping a warm tortilla in a *queso fundido* (cheese fondue). ◈ 8461 SW 132nd St, Pinecrest • Map F4 • 786-242-4444 • $$

7 Two Chefs
American and contemporary cuisine with international influences served in a bistro-style setting. ◈ 8287 South Dixie Highway • Map F4 • 305-663-2100 • $$$$

8 The Melting Pot
A relaxed atmosphere with private tables. The menu ranges from vegetarian dishes to filet mignon. ◈ 11520 SW Sunset Dr • Map F4 • 305-279-8816 • $$$

9 Sushi Maki
Good sushi at reasonable prices. The volcano roll is a creamy, multi-fish treat, or choose from 30 other creative rolls. ◈ 5812 Sunset Dr • Map F4 • 305-667-7677 • $$$

10 Cauley Square Tea Room
A light and lacy setting in a period cottage. Order hot crab-meat au gratin, a large tuna-nut salad, or a shrimp platter. Open for lunch only. ◈ 12310 SW 224th St • Map E5 • 305-258-0044 • $$

Note: Unless otherwise stated, all restaurants have disabled access, accept credit cards, and serve vegetarian meals

Left **Crowd at Key West** Center **Duval Street, Key West** Right **Dolphin Research Center**

The Keys

THE FLORIDA KEYS ARE A STRING OF WILD, *variegated gems hung in a necklace of liquid turquoise. These islands still have abundant wildlife, including unique flora and fauna, as evidenced by all the parks and family attractions focusing on encounters with nature. Even so, at least 20 different species of Keys plant and animal life are endangered or threatened. This is a place for outdoor activities: water sports of all kinds, sportfishing, and hiking through the nature preserves and virgin tropical forests. Along the only route (US 1) that takes you from the mainland all the way out to Key West, you'll find everything from plush resorts to roadside stands selling home-grown produce.*

Key West house

🔟 Sights

1. John Pennekamp Coral Reef State Park
2. Dolphin Cove
3. Theater of the Sea
4. Indian Key Historic State Park
5. Dolphin Research Center
6. Museum of Natural History of the Florida Keys
7. Pigeon Key
8. Bahia Honda State Park
9. Mel Fisher Maritime Museum
10. Key West

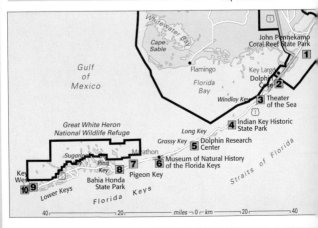

Previous pages **Harbor at Key West**

Jetty, John Pennekamp Park

1 John Pennekamp Coral Reef State Park

The park is best known for its fabulous coral reef life. You can also rent canoes, dinghies, or motorboats, as well as snorkeling and scuba gear, or choose a glass-bottom boat ride. Most destinations are actually located in the neighboring Florida Keys (Key Largo) National Marine Sanctuary. The shallow waters of White Bank Dry Rocks is especially good for snorkeling, as well as nearby Molasses Reef. ◈ MM 102.5 oceanside • Map D5 • 305-451-1202 • 8am–sunset daily • Adm

2 Dolphin Cove

This marine environment research center, set on a lagoon, will literally let you swim with the dolphins for a high fee. You can go in as a non-swimming observer or a lot less money. Other programs include guided kayaking and snorkeling tours, back country eco-tours, and crocodile tours. By contrast, there's also a romantic Champagne Sunset

Cruise on the placid waters of Florida Bay. ◈ MM 101.9 Bayside • Map C5 • 305-451-4060 • 8am–5pm daily • Dolphin swim sessions at 9am, 1pm and 3:30pm Sat & Sun only • Adm • www.dolphinscove.com

3 Theater of the Sea

Did you know that dolphins feel like wet inner tubes and stingrays like Jello (gelatin)? This is the world's second-oldest (since 1946) marine mammal facility and offers a wide variety of shows and programs. There are dolphin and sea lion shows or, if you prefer, you can swim with them here, too. For a big fee, "Swim With the Dolphins" guarantees hugs, dorsal tows, and smooches. "Swim With the Sea Lions" includes flipper tows and hugs, too. "Swim With the Stingrays" is the least expensive. ◈ MM 84.5 oceanside • Map C5 • 305-664-2431 • www.theaterofthesea.com • 9:30am– 4pm daily • Adm

4 Indian Key Historic State Park

Tiny Indian Key has a surprising amount of history for its size (10.5 acres/4.25ha). An ancient Native American site, it was settled in 1831 by Captain J. Houseman, an opportunistic wrecker. In 1840 Seminoles attacked, killing the settlers. The Key was abandoned, and today only the outlines of the village remain, overgrown by vegetation. These are the descendants of plants belonging to Dr. Henry Perrine, a botanist who was killed in the raid. ◈ MM 78.5 oceanside • Map C5 • 305-664-9814 for ferry service • Sunrise–sunset daily

Coral, John Pennekamp Park

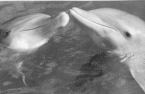

Left **Dolphin Research Center** Right **Dolphins**

5 Dolphin Research Center

A not-for-profit concern, whose main function is to research dolphin behavior and provide a rest home for sick and injured dolphins, or those worn out from theme-park living. There are exhibits, regularly scheduled lagoon-side walking tours, and special programs featuring the Atlantic bottlenose dolphins. "Dolphin Encounter" lets you swim and interact with the creatures. Note that some programs have age or height restrictions and require 30-day advance reservations. ⬥ *MM 59 bayside • Map C6 • 305-289-0002 • www. dolphins.org • 9am–4pm daily • Adm*

6 Museum of Natural History of the Florida Keys

You can see a 600-year-old dugout canoe, remnants of pirate ships, a simulated coral reef cave, and the Bellarmine jug (circa 1580), a shipwreck artifact in almost perfect condition. There's also the Florida Keys Children's Museum and Marathon Wild Bird Center. ⬥ *MM 50.5 bayside • Map B6 • 305-743-9100 • 9am– 5pm Mon–Sat, noon–5pm Sun • Adm*

Shell, Museum of Natural History

7 Pigeon Key

This was originally the site of the work camp for those who

The Keys: Myth and Magic

The very name conjures up visions of windswept seascapes and wild goings-on: Humphrey Bogart and Lauren Bacall in the classic melodrama, *Key Largo*; some of the greatest American writers (Ernest Hemingway, Tennessee Williams, et al.) finding their respective muses where the US meets the Caribbean; and a free, unfettered lifestyle that seems too good to be true.

built Henry M. Flagler's Overseas Railroad Bridge, which was described as the eighth wonder of the world when it was completed in 1912. A marine research foundation has been established in the old buildings. To get to the island, you can walk or take the shuttle, which uses a section of the original bridge. ⬥ *Shuttle depot at MM 47 oceanside • Map B6 • 305-289-0025 • www.pigeon key.org • 9am–5pm daily • Adm*

8 Bahia Honda State Park

This protected area boasts the finest beaches in all the Keys – and is often voted among the best in the US. Brilliantly white sand is backed by dense, tropical forest crossed by a number of nature trails. ⬥ *Bahia Honda Key, Milemarker 37 oceanside • Map B6 • 305-872-2353 • Adm*

Bahia Honda State Park

9 Mel Fisher Maritime Museum

The Mel Fisher Maritime Heritage Society and Museum brings you the Age of Discovery, from the late 15th to the mid-18th centuries, when Europeans explored what was to them the "New World." Their exploits, their commerce, and their impact on the native inhabitants of the Americas can be understood in the artifacts in this museum's collection. It has four ships, including the *St. John's Wreck*, built in 1560, and the *Henrietta Marie*, an English galleon that sank off the Florida Keys in 1700. ◑ *200 Greene Street, Key West • Map A6 • 305-294-2633 • www.melfishermaritime museum.org • 9:30am–5pm daily • Adm*

10 Key West

Rich in history and breath-taking beauty, the self-styled Conch (pronounced "conk") republic seems truly a world apart from the rest of the US (*see pp26–7*).

Duval Street, Key West

A Day's Walk on Key West

Morning

Begin at about 10am. Start at the Southernmost Point in the continental US, over-looking the Atlantic at the intersection of Whitehead and South Streets, where the marker informs you that Cuba is only 90 miles (144 km) away. Then head up Whitehead to the **Lighthouse Museum** and climb its 88 steps for a great overview of the island and beyond.

Next stop is **Hemingway House**, at 907; here you can take in a nostalgic trip through the writer's life as a Conch. Then move on to the **Green Parrot Bar**, at 601 Whitehead, to admire its age-old funkiness and have a drink before lunch. From here, head over to Duval Street, to **Mangoes Restaurant**, at 700, for a great lunch and equally stellar people-watching.

Afternoon

Afterwards, take a look at the Spanish Colonial façade of the **San Carlos Opera House**, and, on the next block up, the stained-glass windows of **St. Paul's Episcopal Church**. At 322, pay a visit to the **Wreckers' Museum**.

Now things might get very "Key West," as you climb to the third floor of The Bull at 224 to find **The Garden of Eden** and see who's sunning themselves in this clothing-optional bar.

Farther along, stop at his-toric **Sloppy Joe's** bar. By now, it should be time for the famous sunset celebra-tion, so head to Mallory Square and add your posi-tive energy to the festivities!

Left **Mangrove, Key Largo Hammocks State Botanical Site** Right **Bahia Honda**

TOP 10 Nature Preserves

1 Key Largo Hammocks Botanical State Park

The largest remaining stand of tropical West Indian hardwood and mangrove is a refuge for protected indigenous flora and fauna. ✪ *1 mile N of US 1, on Route 905, oceanside • 305-451-1202 • 8am–5pm daily, guided tours 10am Thu & Sun • Free*

2 John Pennekamp Coral Reef State Park

Most famous for its stunning offshore coral reef, where snorkeling, scuba diving, and glass-bottom boat rides are great favorites *(see p115)*.

3 Florida Keys Wild Bird Rehabilitation Center

A safe haven for recovering Keys birds of all types. Healed ones are set free, if they like. ✪ *MM 93.6, bayside • 305-852-4486 • Sunrise–sunset daily • Donation*

4 Windley Key Fossil Reef State Geological Site

Nature displays in the center, and trails into the railroad's old quarries, where you can see fossilized brain coral and sea ferns. ✪ *MM 85.5 bayside • 305-664-2540 • 8am–5pm Thu–Mon • Adm*

5 Lignumvitae Key Botanical State Park

Access is by boat only to this virgin hardwood forest home and gardens built by William Matheson. Call the Long Key Recreation Area to arrange a tour. ✪ *MM 78.5 bayside • 305-664-9814 for ferry*

6 Long Key State Park

Features include a boardwalk through a mangrove swamp next to a lagoon where you can see water birds. Snorkeling is good in the shallow waters off the beach. ✪ *MM 67.5 oceanside • 305-664-4815 • 8am–sunset daily • Adm*

7 Crane Point Hammock Museums and Nature Center

Walk the nature trails to Florida Bay and check out the Museum of Natural History of the Florida Keys *(see p116)* and the Adderly Town Historic Site. ✪ *MM 50 bayside • 305-743-9100 • 9am–5pm Mon-Sat, noon–5pm Sun • Adm*

8 Bahia Honda State Park

Very heavily forested, with great nature trails. Fascinating snorkeling, too *(see p117)*.

9 National Key Deer Refuge

Fewer than 50 of these diminutive creatures were left until this refuge was established in 1957. Now there are estimated to be about 800. Drive very slowly. ✪ *MM 30.5 bayside • 305-872-0774 • Sunrise–sunset daily • Free*

10 Florida Keys National Marine Sanctuary

Looe Key Reef is one of the Keys' most spectacular coral reefs and is great for snorkeling and diving. Call for information about boat trips to the best spots. ✪ *MM 27.5 oceanside • 305-292-0311*

Left **Egrets and the rare roseate spoonbill** Right **Endangered American crocodiles**

🔟 Plants and Animals in the Keys

1 Key Deer
The diminutive Key deer (max. 32 in/81 cm tall) are found primarily on Big Pine and No Name keys. Docile and endearing, these tiny animals have returned from the brink of extinction in the last 40 years.

2 Coral
Although it appears to be insensate rock, coral is actually a living organism, and a very fragile one at that, easily damaged by the slightest touch.

3 Gumbo Limbo Tree
This unmistakable tree is found all over the Keys – called the "tourist tree" because its bark is red and peeling.

4 Palms
Although only a few species are natives – the royal palm, the sabal palm, the saw palmetto, and the thatch palm – a huge range of imported palms now adorn the islands.

5 Sea Turtles
These good-natured, long-lived creatures come in a wide variety of shapes and sizes. From the largest to the smallest they are the leatherback, the loggerhead, the green, the hawksbill, and the Ridley turtles.

6 Herons
These elegant birds include the great blue heron (white phase, too), the little blue heron, the tri-colored heron, the green-backed heron, and the black-crowned night heron.

7 Egrets
Similar to herons are the great egret, the snowy egret (distinguishable by its black legs and yellow feet), and the reddish egret.

8 White Ibis
Recognizable for its long, down-curving beak, this medium-sized white bird was sacred to the Egyptians.

9 Double-Crested Cormorant
Notable for its S-curved neck, distinctive beak, and spectacular diving skills, this is one of the most fascinating of Keys birds.

10 Other Endangered Species
These include the American crocodile, the Key Largo wood rat and cotton mouse, Schaus swallowtail butterfly, and roseate spoonbill, all of which have either been hunted to near extinction or lost their habitats due to human encroachment.

Heron in the Keys

Left **Sign for a dive center in the Keys** Center **Parasailing** Right **Sailing**

Sports Activities in the Keys

1 Swimming
Some of the best beaches in the world are found in the Keys. Don't worry if the ocean temperature happens to fall below the usual 79°F (26°C) – most hotels have heated swimming pools.

2 Snorkeling and Scuba Diving
Since the Keys are almost entirely surrounded by America's largest living coral reef, the underwater world is one of the main treats the area has to offer.

3 Fishing
Deep-sea fishermen find the Keys to be paradise. With the Gulf Stream nearby, these waters offer the most varied fishing imaginable. Boat trips are easy to come by; try the Key West Fishing Club. *Fishing Club 305-294-3618 • www.keywestfishingclub.com*

4 Windsurfing
With prevailing winds and calm, shallow waters that remain so for miles out to sea, the Keys are windsurfing perfection. Most moderately busy beaches up and down the islands have shops that rent all the necessary equipment.

5 Parasailing
As close to growing wings as you can get, parasailing in the Keys is easy, safe, and unforgettable. Many small companies offer the experience, such as Sebago, on the Key West Bight. *Sebago 305-292-2411*

6 Bicycling
There is no doubt that bicycling is one of the best ways to see the Keys. The roads are fairly bike-friendly, especially in Key West, and bicycle rentals are readily available.

7 Boating and Sailing
The many dozens of marinas in the Keys are full of companies ready to rent you whatever kind of boat you would like – or to take you out, if you prefer.

8 Water-skiing and Jet-skiing
These more intense ways of enjoying the Keys waters are available wherever there's a marina, especially, of course in Key West and other developed tourist areas. Island Water Sport is one of the companies offering jetskis. *Island Water Sport 305-296-1754*

9 Golf
Golf courses are not as ubiquitous in the Keys as in the rest of Florida, but there are several good ones, for example on Marathon Key at MM 53.5 oceanside or a more expensive course on Key West.

10 Tennis
Good tennis clubs can be found on just about every developed Key – on Islamorada at MM 76.8 bayside, Marathon a MM 53.5 oceanside, on Key West, of course, and elsewhere.

For more on the beaches and watersports in the Keys and around Miami See pp30–35

Left **The Seven-Mile Bridge** Right **Hemingway lookalikes during Hemingway Days**

🔟 Special Tours and Events

1 Conch Tour Train
Key West's train tour is a must-do for first-time visitors. It gives an invaluable overview of the place and all sorts of insights into its history and culture.

2 Dry Tortugas
Take a plane or ferry to this totally undeveloped collection of islands, where the snorkeling is unbeatable (see pp32 & 129).

3 Old Town Ghost Walk
A lantern-lit evening stroll through the mysterious streets of Key's West's Old Town allows you to discover a haunted island. ✆ Tours depart each evening from the Crowne Plaza La Concha Hotel, 450 Duval St

4 Goombay Celebration
A celebration of Island culture and life, with the emphasis on great music. Held in mid-October, it usually merges with the Fantasy Fest (below). ✆ Bahama Village, Key West

5 Fantasy Fest
Held on Key West in October, for at least ten days leading up to and including Halloween, this is the festival with the most fun, positive atmosphere the US has to offer (see p40).

6 Cuban American Heritage Festival
In June, Key West remembers its rich Cuban heritage and celebrates with ethnic foods, terrific music, and dancing in the streets of the island. ✆ 305-295-9665

7 Old Island Days
A tour of gardens and homes held in the first three months of the year, but also an excuse for "Conchs" to celebrate being themselves – something they're always ready to do in Key West. ✆ 305-294-1241

8 Annual Conch-Blowing Contest
Late April is when this traditional means of musical expression – or noise-making in less skilled cases – fills the air over Key West. Expect anything from poetic foghorn-like sounds to pathetic blats. Part of Conch Republic independence celebrations.

9 Seven-Mile Bridge Run
In mid- to late April, enthusiastic runners honor the bridge that joined all the Keys together by conquering it with their own two feet. ✆ Marathon Key • 305-743-5417

10 Hemingway Days
Since it's held in the middle of the low season, the third week of July (Hemingway's birthday was July 21st), this party is mainly for the "Conchs." Consequently, it seems to be the celebration most loved by the locals. Hemingway lookalikes help lead the celebrations and tributes to the island's most famous writer. ✆ 305-294-1136

For more information on special tours and events in the Keys, contact the Key West Vistor Center on 1-800-527-8539

Left **Archaeo** Right **Key West Hand Print**

Island Shopping

1 The Gallery at Kona Kai Resort

Impressive selection of international artwork, including painting (Sobran and Magni), sculpture (Pollès bronzes), and stunning Keys nature photography. ✪ *MM 978 bayside, 97802 Overseas Highway (US 1) • Map C5 • ww.konakairesort.com*

2 Treasure Village

An inviting complex, notable for the giant lobster sculpture outside and a real parrot in the central courtyard, which houses crafts and specialty shops. ✪ *MM 86.7 oceanside, 86729 Old Highway (US 1) • Map C5 • www.hellokeys.com*

3 Archeo

Rare African masks and wood carvings, plus dozens of stunning Persian rugs, make this shop one of the most beautiful in town. ✪ *1208 Duval St, Key West • Map A6 • www.archeogallery.com*

4 Environmental Circus

"Let the flowers grow and the music flow." This delirious shop (est. 1970) is like entering a time warp and returning to the dippy days of hippie hedonism. Headshop apparatus, weird comics, and flower-child fashions. ✪ *518 Duval Street, Key West • Map A6*

5 Key West Aloe

A company that has made their own all-natural products since 1971, without any animal testing. ✪ *540 Greene Street, Key West • Map A6 • www.keywestaloe.com*

6 Cuba! Cuba!

Since Key West is closer to Cuba than to the Florida mainland, it makes sense to find a Cuban crafts shop here, despite the official embargo. Items include handmade boxes, dolls, and paintings. ✪ *814 Duval Street, Key West • Map A6 • www.cubacubastore.com*

7 Key West Hand Print

In one of the few brick buildings that survived the great fire of 1886, this huge store sells hand-printed fabrics and fashions. ✪ *201 Simonton St, Key West • Map A6 • www.keywestfashions.com*

8 Peppers of Key West

A wonderful range of spicy sauces for all purposes – from barbecuing to killing off your enemies. ✪ *602 Greene Street, Key West • Map A6 • www.peppersofkeywest.com*

9 Grand Vin

Great wines from around the world at good prices, and the chance to try many of them by the glass. Sit out on the porch. ✪ *Duval Street, Key West • Map A6*

10 Conch Republic Cigar Factory

"Savor the flavor of paradise" is the motto at this old factory that turns out the next best thing to a genuine Cuban stogie. Prices range from $3 to $10.75 for a single cigar. ✪ *512 Greene Street, Key West • Map A6 • www.conch-cigars.com*

Left **Bourbon Street** Center **La-Te-Da** Right **Graffiti**

🔟 Gay and Lesbian Venues

1 Gay and Lesbian Community Center, Key West
There's always plenty of information here for the taking, as well as occasional events. ◎ 513 Truman Ave, Key West • Map A6 • 305-292-3223 • www.glcckeywest.org

2 Bourbon Street Complex
Included here are the popular Bourbon Street Pub, the 801 Bourbon Bar, 1 Saloon, Magnolia's and Pizza Joe's, and The New Orleans House, a gay guesthouse. 801 features nightly drag shows. ◎ 722-801 Duval Street, Key West • Map A6

3 Atlantic Shores Resort
Right on the water, with its own deck, pool, and pier, they've been sponsoring a Tea Dance every Sunday evening for over 20 years. Clothing always optional. Open to participants of all sexual inclinations. ◎ 510 South Street, Key West • Map A6 • 305-296-2491

4 La-Te-Da
This upscale venue with an excellent restaurant is a popular gay and lesbian spot of long-standing. "Guys as Dolls" and other acts in the Crystal Room Cabaret nightly. ◎ 1125 Duval Street, Key West • Map A6 • 305-296-6706

5 KWEST
Multi-bar complex featuring nightly drag show, men dancing for men, a leather bar and shop, and theme nights. ◎ 705 Duval St, Key West • Map A6 • 305-292-8500

6 Graffiti
Trendy and pricey styles designed with the young gay male in mind. Most of the fashions are understated, but there's also a good selection of flash to suit the mood of this sybaritic island. ◎ 701 Duval Street, Key West • Map A6

7 In Touch
Lots of amusing erotica, cards, sexy clothing, toys, and other same-sex fun stuff for both gay men and lesbians. ◎ 715 Duval Street, Key West • Map A6

8 Fairvilla Megastore
An impressively comprehensive store for gay couples seeking toys, erotic movies, games, and sensual accessories. ◎ 520 Front St, Key West • Map A6

9 Aqua Night Club
This vibrant video club is open every night. Happy hour begins at 2pm and there is karaoke and a drag show. The wet bar out the back has a relaxing and quiet atmosphere with torches and a waterfall. ◎ 711 Duvall Street, Key West • Map A6 • 305-294-0555

10 AIDS Memorial
Squares of black granite are engraved with the names of about a thousand Conchs who have been taken by the disease, along with some poignant, inspirational poetry. ◎ Atlantic Ocean end of White Street • Map A6

→ Exclusively gay and lesbian accommodations are available in Key West – **See p153**

Left **Sloppy Joe's** Right **The Bull**

🔟 Bars, Pubs, and Clubs

1 Sloppy Joe's
You can get a full meal as well as just a drink at this prominently situated and always noisy bar. It's heavy on Hemingway memorabilia, since he used to hang out here as well as at the original Sloppy Joe's (see below). ⊗ 201 Duval St, Key West • Map A6 • 305-294-5717

2 Captain Tony's Saloon
This was the original Sloppy Joe's, where Hemingway was a regular. Live bands feature all the time; Conch hero Jimmy Buffett used to sing here. ⊗ 428 Greene St, Key West • Map A6 • 305-294-1838

3 Green Parrot Bar
Established in 1890 and still going strong. Lots of locals, pool tables, and all kinds of live music on weekends. ⊗ 601 Whitehead St., Key West • Map A6 • 305-294-6133

4 The Bull
Three bars in one, on three different floors. Street level always has some live entertainment, while the top floor open deck is the Garden of Eden, the famous clothing-optional bar (see p49 & p117). ⊗ 224 Duval St, Key West • Map A6 • 305-296-4545

5 Hog's Breath Saloon
One of the best-known bars due to a far-reaching ad campaign – it's part of a Florida chain. Expect lots of heavy drinking and live music. ⊗ 400 Front St, Key West • Map A6 • 305-292-2032

6 Margaritaville
Local-boy-made-good Jimmy Buffett is the owner of this bar-restaurant-souvenir shop. There is live music nightly, and on occasion the Parrot Head leader himself shows up. ⊗ 500 Duval St, Key West • Map A6 • 305-292-1435

7 Top Lounge
Located on the seventh floor of the Crowne Plaza La Concha Hotel, the Top Lounge is one of the best places to get a 360-degree view of the island and beyond, drink in hand. You can also go up for the view when the bar is closed. ⊗ 430 Duval St, Key West • Map A6 • 305-296-2991

8 Schooner Wharf Bar
This bar is located in the Historic Seaport District, offering open-air views of the waterfront and live music. ⊗ 202 William St., Key West • Map A6 • 305-292-9520

9 Rick's Dirty Harry's Entertainment Complex
This complex has 10 bars. Rick's Downstairs has live music, Rick's Upstairs is one of the hottest dance clubs in town. ⊗ 202 Duval St, Key West • Map A6 • 305-296-4890

10 Berlin's Cigar and Cocktail Bar
Paneled walls, thick carpet, and soft lights create old-world charm here. Have a cigar and a cocktail while enjoying the view of yachts at Key West Bight. ⊗ 700 Front St, Key West • Map A6 • 305-294-5880

Price Categories

For a three course meal for one with half a bottle of wine (or equivalent meal), taxes, and extra charges.

$	under $20
$$	$20–$40
$$$	$40–$55
$$$$	$55–$80
$$$$$	over $80

Mangoes

TOP 10 Conch Dining

1 A & B Lobster House
Located in the heart of Key West in a renovated historic building. Maine lobster, fresh shrimp, and waterfront views. ◎ *700 Front St, Key West • Map A6 • 305-294-5880 • $$$$*

2 Rick's Blue Heaven
You'll never forget the charm and delicious food at this wonderful place *(see p26)*.

3 Mangoes
A meal here is not to be missed, not only for the exciting food – such as their signature wild mushroom and truffle "martini" – but also because the place is so central to Key West life. ◎ *700 Duval St, Key West • Map A6 • 305-292-4606 • $$$*

4 Louie's Backyard
Haute cuisine in a breezy, easy setting right on the Atlantic. Enticing menu items include arugula and spinach with sweet-hot mustard vinaigrette and crispy duck wontons, and knock-out desserts. ◎ *700 Waddell Ave, Key West • Map A6 • 305-294-1062 • $$$$$*

5 One Duval
The chef utilizes the abundance of ingredients indigenous to the Caribbean and the Florida peninsula, preparing them with a flourish that redefines regional cuisine. The lobster with marinated plantain is delicious. ◎ *Pier House Resort, 1 Duval St, Key West • Map A6 • 305-296-4600 • $$$$*

6 El Siboney
Great Cuban food in abundance in a friendly, no-nonsense setting. Lots of diversity, such as roast pork with casava and *tamale*, breaded *palomilla* steak, or stuffed crab. ◎ *900 Catherine St, Key West • Map A6 • 305-296-4184 • $$*

7 Duval Beach Club
Owned by actress Kelly McGillis, this restaurant-snack bar is easy-going and pleasant, serving mostly sandwiches, salads, and great breakfasts. ◎ *1405 Duval St, Key West • Map A6 • 305-295-6550 • $$$*

8 Awful Arthur's
Great oysters, crab legs, spicy steamed peel-and-eat shrimp, clams, mussels, crawfish, conch fritters, and Island rum drinks to wash it down. ◎ *On Angela St, right off Duval • Map A6 • 305-293-7663 • $$$*

9 Camille's
Homemade buckwheat pancakes or fresh snapper with a nut crust help make this a favorite for Sunday brunch. ◎ *1202 Simonton St, Key West • Map A6 • 305-296-4811 • $$$*

10 Mangia Mangia Pasta Café
Open for lunch and dinner, this central Italian eatery has superb fresh pasta. As a result, it's always busy and a firm local favorite. Tasty sauces, and great lasagne. ◎ *900 Southard St, Key West • Map A6 • 305-294-2469 • $$$*

Note: Unless otherwise stated, all restaurants have disabled access, accept credit cards, and serve vegetarian meals

125

Left **Boutique, Palm Beach** Center **The Jungle Queen, Fort Lauderdale** Right **Alligator**

Side Trips

IF YOU VENTURE OUT OF THE *more touristed confines of Greater Miami, be ready for some mild culture shock.* Not only is the rough-and-ready Native American way of life on the Everglades reservations apparent, but even the Gulf Coast and Treasure Coast enclaves can seem to exist in a world apart. Gone entirely is the international feel, and in its place is a sense of the old Florida.

Side Trips

1. A1A North Along the Gold Coast
2. The Everglades, across Alligator Alley (I-75)
3. The Everglades, across the Tamiami Trail (Hwy 41)
4. Loxahatchee National Wildlife Refuge
5. A1A North Along the Treasure Coast
6. Naples and Around
7. Fort Myers
8. Sanibel and Captiva Islands
9. Dry Tortugas from Key West
10. Lake Okeechobee

Via Roma, Palm Beach

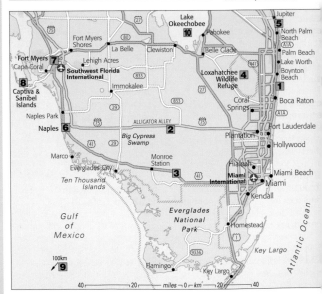

View of the Gold Coast

its inception has been called the Tamiami Trail, which sounds like a Native American word but simply stands for Tampa-Miami, the cities connected by the road. However, it does take you deep into Seminole country, where you can experience the wonders of the Everglades. As you make your way to the Gulf coast, be sure to stop at Everglades City and Naples *(see p128)*. ⊗ *Map A3–C4*

1 A1A North along the Gold Coast

Starting just at the northern tip of Miami Beach is a stretch of beautiful, wealthy communities that goes on for at least 50 miles (80 km). As diverse in their own ways as the Greater Miami area, they add immeasurably to the cultural richness of South Florida and make an unsurpassed choice for beaching it, too *(see pp24–5)*.

2 The Everglades, across Alligator Alley (I-75)

This is probably the easiest, fastest route across the Everglades: an Interstate toll-road with two lanes of traffic in each direction. It keeps you at arm's length from the swampy, teeming mass of it all, but there are several great stops along the way, as you pass through Big Cypress National Preserve and just to the north of Fakahatchee Strand State Preserve. ⊗ *Map B–C3*

3 The Everglades, across the Tamiami Trail (Hwy 41)

Highway 41 was the first cut across the Everglades and from

4 Loxahatchee National Wildlife Refuge

This is the only surviving remnant of the northern Everglades, a vast area of mostly sawgrass marsh that is so characteristic of the Everglades environment. The inviting public-use areas provide viewing opportunities for a large variety of wetland flora and fauna, including egrets, alligators, and the endangered snail kite. Activities include nature walks, hiking, canoeing, bird-watching, and bass-fishing. A 5-mile (8-km) canoe trail provides the best way to see and explore the refuge up close. ⊗ *10216 Lee Road, Boynton Beach • Map C–D 2–3 • 1-800-683-5873 • Sunrise–sunset daily • Adm*

Birdlife, the Everglades

 For more on the Everglades See pp28–9

Fountain, Palm Beach

5 A1A North along the Treasure Coast

Palm Beach, on the Gold Coast, is the winter playground and shopping mecca of the rich (see p25). If you continue on A1A north of Palm Beach, the megalopolis gives way to the smaller, quieter towns of the Treasure Coast. These include Vero, the largest; Jupiter, which has no barrier islands; Stuart, with its charming historic district; rural-feeling Fort Pierce; and, at the northern extension of the Treasure Coast, the little fishing village of Sebastian. Vist these if you want to experience South Florida beach life without the hurly-burly of Miami. ◈ Map D1–2

Tiffany Co. clock, Palm Beach

6 Naples and Around

If you cross the Everglades, your inevitable first stop on the Gulf Coast will be Naples. This wealthy beach city prides itself on a manicured beauty, 55 golf courses, and a soigné downtown area. There's a pleasant pier where you can commune with pelicans or do some fishing, and 10 miles (16 km) of pristine, sugary beaches, with warmer waters than the Atlantic. Nearby Marco Island, the most northerly of the Ten Thousand Islands archipelago, is a good base for delving into the western fringe of the Everglades. It has been the source of significant Calusa Native American finds, some dating back 3,500 years. ◈ Map A3

7 Fort Myers

Though the town is historically famous as the base of operations for the 19th-century inventor Thomas Alva Edison, modern Fort Myers has become one of the main escapes for Mid-westerners seeking a holiday by the sea, especially in winter. Its beaches have the feel of Indiana or Iowa about them, full of families without any of the Miami obsessions with style. The only problems you're likely to encounter are traffic snarls. ◈ Map A2

The beach and pier at Naples

Historical mansion, Fort Myers

8 Sanibel and Captiva Islands

The Lee Island Coast offers an irresistible combination of sandy beaches, exotic wildlife, lush vegetation, and wonderful sunsets. The jewels in the crown are Sanibel and Captiva Islands, which offer a Caribbean-style laid-back atmosphere mixed with upscale shops and restaurants. Much of the territory is protected, and development has been limited: there are no condos and very few large hotels, mainly just houses and cottages scattered among the greenery. ◈ Map A3

9 Dry Tortugas from Key West

You can travel to the wonderful islands of the Dry Tortugas by seaplane or ferry from Key West. Companies offering trips include the Yankee Freedom and the Fast Cat. The day-long tours include food and snorkeling gear. Camping overnight is also possible. The most visited island is Garden Key, the site of Fort Jefferson (see also p32). ◈ Map A5 • Yankee Freedom, 305-294-7009 • Fast Cat 1-800-236-7937

10 Lake Okeechobee

This huge lake – the name means "big water" in the language of the Native American Seminoles – is the second largest

The South Florida Land-Rush

South Florida's warm winter climate and economic upswing of the early 20th century made it seem a perfect place to build the American Dream. The 1920s saw South Florida's first great land boom, when rampant development threatened to make the Everglades a memory. At the height of the boom, prime land could fetch $26,000 per acre, but many would-be investors were bankrupted after being scammed into buying swampland far from the waterfront. The bubble definitively burst with the one-two punch of a hurricane in 1926 and the Great Depression a few years later.

freshwater lake in the US, covering 750 sq miles (1,942 sq km). Though not particularly scenic because of a high dike that was built all the way around it, it is well known for its excellent fishing opportunities. The towns around the lake are relatively undeveloped for tourism, some even rather grim. The best to use as a fishing base is pleasant little Clewiston. The main industry south of the lake is sugar cane – growers are often at odds with environmentalists who are trying to preserve the Everglades. ◈ Map C2

Fort Jefferson, Dry Tortugas

Price Categories

For a three-course	
meal for one with half	**$** under $20
a bottle of wine (or	**$$** $20–$40
equivalent meal), taxes,	**$$$** $40–$55
and extra charges.	**$$$$** $55–$80
	$$$$$ over $80

Alice's at La-Te-Da

🔟 Where to Eat

1 Le Café de Paris, Fort Lauderdale

This family-owned French restaurant has been around for more than 30 years, offering good food and good value. The escargot appetizer is especially delicious. ◈ *715 East Las Olas Blvd, Fort Lauderdale • Map D3 • 954-467-2900 • $$$*

2 Swamp Water Café, Everglades

Genuine swamp food: alligator tail nuggets, catfish filets, frog-legs, and even some local venison. ◈ *Big Cypress Reservation, 20 miles north at exit 14 off I-75 from Ft Lauderdale or Naples • Map B3 • 1-800-949-6101 • $$*

3 Rod and Gun Club, Everglades

Set in a classic Florida frontier hotel, with great views. Fresh fish sandwiches (soft-shell crab or succulent grouper) a specialty. ◈ *200 Riverside Dr, Everglades City • Map B4 • 239-695-2101 • No credit cards • No vegetarian options • $$$*

4 Café Protegé, West Palm Beach

A gourmet restaurant on the campus of a great culinary school. Try the escargot in a garlic and white wine cream sauce. ◈ *2410 Metrocenter Blvd, West Palm Beach • Map D2 • 561-687-2433 • $$$*

5 Sinclair's Ocean Grill, Jupiter

Indoor or patio dining. The cuisine is traditional Floribbean – a bit of Caribbean, Pacific Rim, and Floridian. ◈ *Jupiter Beach Resort, 5 North A1A, Jupiter • Map D2 • 561-745-7120 • $$$*

6 The Dock at Crayton Cove, Naples

More Floribbean crossover cuisine, with macadamia fried goat cheese and Jamaican jerk chicken quesadilla. ◈ *845 12th Ave S at Naples Bay • Map A3 • 239-263-9940 • $$$$*

7 The Veranda, Fort Myers

Charming restaurant, with Deep South décor. The artichoke fritter stuffed with blue crab is outstanding. ◈ *2122 2nd St, Fort Myers • Map A2 • 239-332-2065 • $$$$*

8 Key Lime Bistro, Captiva

Fun and funky, with a beachy feel. Dishes include a tri-color vegetarian terrine and chicken voodoo. Sunday jazz brunch, too. ◈ *11509 Andy Rosse Lane, Captiva Island • Map A3 • 239-395-4000 • $$$$*

9 Alice's at La-Te-Da, Key West

Alice Weingarten creates culinary magic, with her signature fusion cuisine, all set in a romantic garden atmosphere. ◈ *1125 Duval St, Key West • Map A6 • 305-296-6706 • $$$$*

10 Colonial Dining Room, Clewiston

Fresh fish from Lake Okeechobee, and a genteel air. Antiques and antebellum-style reproductions abound. ◈ *Clewiston Inn, 108 Royal Palm Ave • Map C2 • 863-983-8151 • $$$*

Key West is included here as the access point for the Dry Tortugas – for more Key West restaurants **See p125**

Price Categories

For a standard double room per night (with breakfast if included), taxes, and extra charges.

$	under $100
$$	$100–$200
$$$	$200–$250
$$$$	$250–$300
$$$$$	over $300

Left **Hyatt Regency** Right **Jupiter Beach Resort**

TOP 10 Where to Stay

1 Hyatt Regency Pier 66, Fort Lauderdale

Fantastic views from the revolving Pier Top Lounge. Well-appointed rooms, and facilities include a spa and fitness center. ◈ 2301 SE 17th St Causeway, Fort Lauderdale • Map D3 • 1-888-591-1234 • www.hyatt.com • $$$$

2 Billie Swamp Safari Wildlife Park, Everglades

The amenities are little better than camping out, but this is a chance to get up close and personal with the Everglades. ◈ Big Cypress Reservation • Map B3 • 1-800-949-6101 • www.seminoletribe.com • No private baths or air conditioning • $

3 Rod and Gun Lodge, Everglades

Resting quietly in the Everglades, but with a colorful past that includes stays by Hemingway, US presidents, and even Mick Jagger. ◈ 200 Riverside Dr, Everglades City • Map B4 • 239-695-2101 • No credit cards • $$

4 Hibiscus House, West Palm Beach

Victorian décor, exquisite china, and individually outfitted rooms, plus an outstanding pool and patio area. ◈ 501 30th St, West Palm Beach • Map D2 • 1-800-203-4927 • www.hibiscushouse.com • $$

5 Jupiter Beach Resort

Plush but unpretentious. The rooms are simple but have marble baths, colorful furnishings, and (mostly) terrific views. Good choice for families. ◈ 5 North A1A, Jupiter • Map D2 • 1-800-228-8810 • www.jupiterbeachresort.com • $$$

6 The Inn on Fifth, Naples

Cozy hotel radiating Mediterranean charm, with lavish fountains and plush interiors. ◈ 699 5th Ave S, Naples • Map A3 • 1-888-403-8778 • www.naplesinn.com • $$$$

7 Sanibel Harbour Resort and Spa

Stucco walls, spacious rooms, and a spectacular recreational area, featuring waterfalls and a private beach. ◈ 17260 Harbour Pointe Drive • Map A3 • 1-800-767-7777 • www.sanibel-resort.com • $$$$$

8 Captiva Island Inn

A collection of wood-frame cottages, set among tropical palms and just steps from a faultless beach. ◈ 11509 Andy Rosse Lane, Captiva Island • Map A3 • 1-800-454-9898 • www.captivaislandinn.com • $$

9 Crowne Plaza La Concha, Key West

Tennessee Williams is said to have written A Streetcar Named Desire here; presidents and royalty have stayed, too. ◈ 430 Duval St, Key West • Map A6 • 1-800-745-2191 • www.laconchakeywest.com • $$$$

10 Clewiston Inn

Evokes a pre-Civil War atmosphere with its décor. ◈ 108 Royal Palm Ave • Map C2 • 1-800-749-4466 • www.clewistoninn.com • $$

For the main listing of hotels in Miami and the Keys
See pp146–53

STREETSMART

Planning Your Trip
134

Sources of Information
135

Tips for Arriving in Miami
136

Tips for Getting Around
Miami
137

Media Sources
138

Ways to Stay
Healthy and Safe
139

Things to Avoid
140

Money and
Communication Tips
141

Ways to Save Money
142

Senior and Disabled
Travelers
143

Hotlines and Helplines
144

Accommodation Tips
145

Places to Stay
146–153

MIAMI'S TOP 10

Left **Downtown Miami**

TOP 10 Planning Your Trip

1 When to Go/Climate

With its subtropical climate, South Florida is a year-round destination. However, late spring and summer can be uncomfortably hot, with rain showers almost every afternoon. The high season is from about December to April.

2 Length of Stay

Stay as long as possible. Besides the beach life, South Florida has a great deal to offer, especially in high season, when there seems to be a festival just about every week. Many hotels offer special deals if you stay by the week.

3 What to Bring

If coming from abroad, bring an international driver's license, a voltage converter, and any special prescription medicines you need. Also bring some good walking shoes, or, better yet, sandals. Otherwise, bring as little as possible.

Consulates in Miami

- UK 305-374-1522
- Canada 305-579-1600
- Germany 305-358-0290
- France 305-350-0729
- Italy, 305-374-6322
- The Netherlands (786) 866-0480
- Spain 305-446-5511
- Israel 305-925-9400
- Japan 305-530-9090

4 Visas and Passports

Visa regulations may change without notice so it is always best to check before you travel. See www.USCIS.gov for information. Canadians need to show only proof of residence. You may need to be able to prove that you have sufficient funds to cover your stay, and, of course, you must have a return ticket.

5 Customs

Allowances for visitors over 21 years of age entering the US are: 1 liter (2 pints) of alcohol, gifts worth up to $100, and 200 cigarettes, 100 cigars (but not Cuban!), or 3 lbs (1.4 kg) of tobacco. A number of goods are prohibited, including cheese, fresh fruit, meat products, and, of course, illegal drugs.

6 Money and Travel Insurance

Travel insurance is essential for foreign visitors – a minimum of $1 million of medical coverage, including accidental death and emergency care, trip cancellation, and baggage or document loss. Travel with as little cash as you can manage, for safety reasons and to avoid questioning by customs officers.

7 Embassies and Consulates

Most major countries have diplomatic offices in Miami. Most consulates are set up to help their nationals if they run into difficulties.

8 Guided Package Tours

Given Miami's dangerous reputation – though considerably improved of late – many travelers prefer to visit as part of an organized group. This can save a great deal of doubt and stress by answering many questions for you in advance. However, be aware that this type of tour tends to put you up in the least appealing parts of town. Choose a group tour that gives you a maximum of flexibility.

9 Weights, Measures, and Time

The US uses the imperial system of ounces, pounds, inches, feet, yards, miles, etc. (This book gives both imperial and metric values.) Voltage is 110-115 volts, and the electrical plugs have two flat prongs. Miami is in the Eastern Time Zone, five hours behind Greenwich Mean Time, and 3 hours ahead of California.

10 Language

Though English is widely spoken in the main tourist areas, bear in mind that the majority of Miamians speak Spanish as their first language. It is worth learning some basic Spanish phrases as a matter of courtesy.

Left **Miami Chamber of Commerce** Center **Key West Chamber of Commerce** Right **Deco Center**

🔟 Sources of Information

1 Greater Miami & Beaches Convention & Visitors' Bureau
The Bureau has both local and international offices, and a website. It offers maps and pointers to everything in the Greater Miami area, including the Keys and the Everglades.

2 General Tips
The Visit Florida and MetroGuide Miami websites are worth a visit.

3 Chambers of Commerce in Miami
Miami Beach, Coral Gables, and Coconut Grove have their own Chambers of Commerce, which offer local maps and information.

4 Art Deco Welcome Center
Guided tours and self-guided tours (including audioguides) are available, as well as literature on the District and Deco style.

5 Tropical Everglades Visitor Association
Tips on tours and walks, fishing and boating, diving and snorkeling, sights and attractions, restaurants and lodgings.

6 Greater Homestead/Florida City Chamber of Commerce
Provides brochures and discount coupons for the entire South Miami and Everglades area. The office is housed in a period building with a photo exhibit recounting the history of Homestead. The suggested walk around the historic center is worthwhile.

7 Greater Fort Lauderdale Convention & Visitors Bureau
For information about Fort Lauderdale, Hollywood, Pompano Beach, Sunrise, Lauderdale-By-The-Sea, or Deerfield Beach.

8 Vacation Planner Magazine
The free glossy magazine *Vacation Planner*, covering the South Florida area, is available at many information centers.

9 Information About Palm Beach
The Palm Beach Country Convention & Visitors' Bureau has a boatload of materials. Its Chamber of Commerce also publishes an extensive *Official Guide to Palm Beach*.

🔟 Information About Key West
The Monroe County Tourist Development Council – The Florida Keys & Key West – people know everything about the archipelago, and their love for the area is infectious. They provide the best maps and the top tips for getting the most out of every single mile marker along the way.

Directory

Greater Miami CAVB
701 Brickell Ave, Suite 2700, Miami • 1-800-933-8448 • 0171-978-5233 (UK) • www.miami andbeaches.com

General Tips
www.flausa.com • www. miami.metroguide.net

Chambers of Commerce in Miami
1920 Meridian Ave, Miami Beach, 305-672-1270 • 2333 Ponce de Leon Blvd, Colonade Office Tower, Suite 650, Coral Gables, 305-446-1657 • Peacock Park, nr S Bayshore Drive, Coconut Grove, 305-444-7270

Art Deco Center
1001 Ocean Drive
• 305-531-3484
• www.mdpl.org

Everglades (TEVA)
160 US Hwy 1, Florida City • 1-800-388-9669
• www.tropicalever glades.com

Greater Homestead
41-43 North Krome Ave
• 305-242-4814

Fort Lauderdale
1850 Eller Drive, Suite 303 • 1-800-227-8669

Palm Beach
1555 Palm Beach Lakes Blvd • 561-233-3000

Florida Keys
1201 White St, Key West • 305-296-1552
• 01564-794999 (UK)
• www.fla-keys.com

Left **Miami Airport terminal** Center **Shuttle bus** Right **Bridge in the Keys**

TOP 10 Tips for Arriving in Miami

1 Airlines
Several major international and regional airlines serve the Greater Miami area, among them American, Continental, Delta, United, US Airways, AirTran, and Southwest; and from the UK, British Airways, Northwest, and Virgin Atlantic.

2 Airfares
The airline market in the US is quite volatile, with newcomers entering it every year, so bargains can be found – especially with a little time spent searching the Internet. Currently, for domestic flights, AirTran and Southwest are good. Flying mid-week is usually cheaper.

3 Miami International Airport
One of the busiest in the world, which can mean long lines at immigration. There may be lots of walking to do, too. There are tourist information desks and car rental counters outside the customs area, but they are not always staffed when you need them.

4 Fort Lauderdale-Hollywood International Airport
This is the area's second airport, less crowded but just as convenient and served by almost as many airlines as Miami Airport. It's the perfect choice if you're staying along the southern part of the Gold Coast.

5 Car Rental, Taxis, and Shuttle Buses
Options for getting from the airports into Miami are numerous: rental cars, shuttle services (see below), taxis, limousines, and shuttle buses to the Metrorail and TriRail lines.

6 SuperShuttle
This company, and other competitors, offers 24-hour door-to-door service for much less than the cost of a taxi. The catch is that you have to share with other travelers, so you may have to ride around for a bit while others are picked up or dropped off. You can book your pick-up on their website.

7 By Car
The major Interstates that lead to Miami are I-95, down the north coast, and I-75, from the Gulf coast. There's also Florida's Turnpike, which shoots down from Central Florida. These highways are well maintained, with welcome centers along the way. Highways 1, A1A, and 41 are not efficient choices unless you're exploring the Greater Miami area.

8 By Sea
The Port of Miami is, quite simply, the largest in the world. From here endless mammoth cruise ships depart for romantic Caribbean adventures. People arriving by private yacht have a choice of excellent marinas.

9 By Train
Amtrak serves Miami from everywhere in the US. Sleepers and restaurant service are available. For train service within the Miami area, there's the excellent Tri-Rail, which hooks up with the Metrorail system up and down the Gold Coast.

10 By Bus
There's a bus station near the airport and one Downtown, at 100 NW 6th St, served by Greyhound, Trailways, and Metrobus. The buses are cheap but not very convenient if you have much luggage. Greyhound is a decent, though fairly slow, option for getting from Miami to Key West.

Directory

Miami International Airport
305-876-7000

Fort Lauderdale/ Hollywood Airport
954-359-1200

Palm Beach Airport
561-471-7412

SuperShuttle
1-800-258-3826 or 305-871-2000 • www.super shuttle.com

Tri-Rail
1-800-874-7245

Amtrak Railroad
1-800-872-7245

Greyhound and Trailways Bus
1-800-231-2222 for both

Left **Metromover** Center **Cyclists** Right **Vehicles to rent**

ᴛᴏᴘ10 Tips for Getting Around Miami

1 Metrobus System
The Metrobus routes cover the whole Miami-Dade area, but don't expect them to hold to any schedule, or to come even once every hour. You'll need the correct change, a token, or a Metropass.

2 Metrorail and Metromover
Metrorail is a 21-mile (34-km) elevated rail system running from Hialeah in the north to Dadeland in the south. It serves Downtown, Coconut Grove, and Coral Gables. Metromover is a monorail extension of Metrorail that runs a circuit around Downtown *(see p86)*.

3 South Beach Local
This is a fast, scenic way to get around South Beach. There are two separate routes, via Collins and Washington avenues. The cars are air-conditioned and smooth.

4 Taxis and Water Taxis
Taxi meters start at $1.50 and click away speedily at $2 a mile, so they're not a good deal for long distances. In Fort Lauder-dale you may well decide to try a water taxi, just for the fun of exploring the "Venice of America."

5 Skate, Bicycle, and Scooter Rental
These zippy modes of transportation are

definitely the top choices for "doing" South Beach. Many stores will suggest self-guided tours and offer free skating lessons. If you want to ride the American Dream, rent a motorbike.

6 Rental Cars
Car rental in Florida can be expensive, but you can get better deals by looking for fly-drive packages, or by booking through the Internet in advance of your arrival. You'll need a valid driver's license, photo ID, and a credit card (cash or a debit card are rarely accepted). Watch out for hidden extras.

7 Road Rules
Freeways and toll-roads in Miami are gene-rally good and fairly easy to negotiate, but the local drivers are another thing. Lane-changing at top speeds is a local sport, as are all sorts of other erratic habits. The result can be myriad fender-benders and some terrible traffic snarls.

8 Tours
There are tours all over Miami, some even include the Everglades, Fort Lauderdale, or a cruise. See www.key2miami.com for more information.

9 Limousines
Being a star-studded place, stretch limos are a common sight here, the longer the better.

10 Navigation
The grid system of road orientation and numbers (NW, SE, 1st, 2nd, Ave, St, etc) begins Downtown, with Flagler Street as one axis and Miami Avenue as the other. Confusingly, Miami Beach has its own system, as does Coral Gables, and many streets have one or even two extra names.

Directory

Miami-Dade Metro Transit
305-770-3131

Metrobus System
305-770-3131

South Beach Local
305-770-3131

Miami Taxis
305-444-4444, 305-888-8888, or 305-888-7777

Fort Lauderdale Water Taxi
954-467-6677

Bike and Roll
760 Washington St
• 773-276-4400

Harley Rentals
1-888-736-8433

Travel A Plus
305-759-0044
• www.travelaplus.com

Limousines
• Red Carpet Transport-ation, 305-444-4635
• Carey Limousine Service, 305-893-9850
• Limousines of South Florida, 305-940-5252

Left **The Miami Herald** Center **Mallory Square event, Key West** Right **Drop bins, Palm Beach**

Media Sources

1 The Miami Herald
This daily newspaper is Florida's largest, and its weekly supplements *The Street* and *Weekend* are major sources of information about local entertainment and events.

2 Miami New Times
This is the main free alternative weekly, which you can pick up in many restaurants, stores, clubs, and drop bins all over town. It reviews restaurants, movies, clubs, etc.

3 Key West
The island's eponymous weekly newspaper features news about upcoming events, arts, theater, attractions, music, clubs, local news, features, and opinions. And like all true Conch undertakings, it's notoriously iconoclastic, taking on the local police and other authorities in articles.

4 El Nuevo Herald
This is Miami's Spanish-language edition, which naturally focuses more on issues and events relating to the huge Hispanic community.

5 Hotel Magazines
In the "tonier" hotels, you'll often find *Ocean Drive* and *Where*. The former is not much more than a super-stylish fashion vehicle. *Where* is an international publication – the Miami version, which comes out monthly, has some excellent basic insights and even some captivating articles. Note, however, that all the restaurant listings are there because the owners paid to be included, rendering the reviews less than entirely genuine.

6 Network TV
The programming of the main national networks are carried by four Miami channels: Channel 4 is CBS, Channel 6 is NBC, Channel 7 is FOX, and Channel 10 is ABC. Unless your TV is connected to cable, this will be the configuration for receiving all the regularly scheduled sitcoms, sports, and news programming. The PBS station is normally Channel 2.

7 Cable TV
Most TVs you encounter in Miami will be connected to one cable company or another. Most likely this will mean that you receive not only the major networks but also CNN and MSNBC for news, ESPN for sports, the Weather Channel, Comedy Central, and Nickelodeon (for the kids). You might also be lucky enough to get all or some of the innovative HBO programming, as well as excellent Showtime offerings.

8 English FM Radio
Miami may seem mostly Spanish-speaking, but when you turn on the radio, you'll find that most of the banter is still in English. There's the usual big-city mix of country, oldies, new rock, hard rock, jazz, and NPR (National Public Radio) programming and similar local stations, for people who want to hear the topics of the day intelligently considered by interesting thinkers.

9 Spanish FM Radio
There are, of course, several Spanish-language stations, featuring very high-energy programming and the compelling, non-stop rhythms of every sort of Latin American music, from more or less traditional to the very latest international Latino heartthrobs. It's not a bad way to practice your Spanish, particularly because some of the time the announcers are speaking an easy mixture of Spanish and English, often called Spanglish.

10 AM Radio
Since the quality of the FM signal is so much better – and allows for true stereophonic broadcasting – the AM dial in Miami is given over almost entirely to talk radio. Listeners call in to let off steam about whatever topic of the day the commentator has selected to get everyone worked up about. There are both English and Spanish talk radio stations in Miami.

Left **Emergency Room sign** Center **Shades in the sun** Right **Lifeguard**

TOP10 Ways to Stay Healthy and Safe

1 Emergency Numbers

The emergency number 911 is toll free, including from payphones.

2 Security Measures

Always keep your antennae out for potential trouble *(see p140)*. Park in well-lit areas, and keep doors locked and windows closed while driving. Make sure you know where you're going, or at least give that impression. Don't go into uncertain neighborhoods at night.

3 Mugging

If you follow the basic precautions, you're unlikely even to come close to being mugged violently, but do watch out for less aggressive crime. Pickpockets work the crowds, so keep valuables tucked away.

4 Walk-in Medical Services

Most area hospitals operate 24-hour emergency rooms, and there are a number of walk-in clinics. Look in the *Yellow Pages* under "Clinics." You can find 24-hour pharmacies in most areas.

5 Sunburn

The sun is intense here, especially when near the reflective beach and water. Wear sunblock or at least sunscreen at all times, and a hat. Avoid heatstroke by drinking plenty of liquids

and knowing when it's time to head for shade.

6 Insects

Biting and stinging insects, including annoying mosquitoes, can be a real nuisance between June and November. Wear insect repellent, especially when striking out for the Everglades. Other nasty critters are sand flies, which bite in the evening, and fire ants.

7 Riptides and Undertows

Some areas along the Atlantic have rough surf or are subject to strong currents. Small children, in particular, might be better off in some of the more protected waters away from the ocean, especially the gentle Keys waters.

8 Jellyfish, Stingrays, and Sharks

Stinging jellyfish, in particular the man-o-war, sometimes frequent the waters off the coast. Be careful of the ones washed up on the shore, too. Shark attacks are thankfully quite rare. Stingrays are generally gentle creatures, but be careful not to accidentally tread on one.

9 Hurricanes

Hurricanes are infrequent but devastating. If one should occur, follow the announcements on TV and radio, or call the National Hurricane Center.

10 Lost Property

Even though you have only a slim chance of retrieving lost property, report all lost or stolen items to the police. Keep a copy of the police report to claim insurance later. Most credit card companies have toll-free numbers for reporting a loss, as do traveler's check companies *(see p141)*. If you lose a passport, contact your embassy or consulate *(see p134)*.

Directory

Any Emergency
911

Dentist Referrals
305-667-3647

Clinics
Miami Beach Medical Clinic, 1540 Washington Ave, 305-532-4122 • Today's Woman Medical Center, 3250 S Dixie Hwy, Coconut Grove, 305-441-0304

Hospitals:
Beach Community Hospital, 630 Alton, South Beach, 305-672-2100 • Mercy Hospital, 3663 S Miami Ave, Coconut Grove, 305-854-4400 • Coral Gables Hospital, 3100 Douglas Rd, 305-445-8461

National Hurricane Center
305-229-4470

Miami Airport Lost and Found
305-876-7377

For special hotlines and helplines See p144

Left **Respite from the scorching sun** Center **Remember to tip the concierge** Right **Law enforcer**

TOP 10 Things to Avoid

1 Bad Neighborhoods
Most of these areas are in the northern part of Greater Miami, but be aware that just two to three blocks from popular Coco Village, the so-called "Black Grove" is unfortunately quite rundown and dangerous.

2 Bigotry
In outlying areas, outside the bubbles of Miami Beach, Greater Miami and Key West sophistication, you suddenly find yourself in Old Florida, where values can still be quite prejudicial if you are in any way "alternative."

3 Age Restrictions
Ordering alcoholic beverages in a bar if you are under 21, and having alcohol on the beach at any age are strictly prohibited. Needless to say, drunk driving is also entirely unacceptable – often roadblocks are set up on causeways leaving Miami Beach to nab suspicious drivers.

4 Smoking
Buying tobacco if you are under 18 is against the law in Florida. Not that it makes much difference if you're a smoker, as smoking in public buildings is illegal, and they're also considering making it illegal to smoke in bars. All restaurants are non-smoking and many hotels are entirely non-smoking.

5 Forgetting to Tip
Tipping is not an option in the US. Waiters and waitresses get minimum wage or less in the US and depend on whatever tips they clear. Very rarely, the gratuity will be automatically added to your bill, so check. If not, 15 percent of the total before taxes for lunch, and 20 percent for dinner is considered about right.

6 Looking Like a Tourist
To avoid the dangers of pick-pocketing, as well as the nuisance of being accosted by the occasional panhandler, try not to appear to be lost, and don't load yourself down with too much stuff, such as bags, cameras, maps, etc. How you dress is really not such an issue here, as everyone tends to dress down – lots of men even go shirtless all over South Beach streets. One thing that's a definite fashion no-no, however, is wearing socks with your sandals.

7 Forgetting Your Sunscreen
If you didn't bring any sunscreen or sunblock with you, go out immediately and buy a good one. Sunburn is the number one health hazard here, and the sun will get you, you are not an exception. Be sure to apply sunscreen liberally and often, especially to the exposed areas you tend to overlook. If you go to the nude beaches, that advice goes double!

8 The Velvet Rope
Standing in line at a popular club can be a real drag – and you might not get in at all. Talk to your hotel concierge about getting you into the VIP lounge of the club of your choice. For a little extra money, you can save yourself a lot of time and potential disappointment.

9 Law Enforcement
Getting on the wrong side of the Miami cops is never a good idea. There are three separate law enforcement agencies here – city police, county sheriffs, and the highway patrol, and they are generally friendly and helpful, in the spirit of promoting Miami's image as a tourist mecca. However, in the same spirit, if they suspect you are a trouble-maker, they can be notoriously harsh.

10 AIDS
Sex without a condom in this pleasure-loving area is a really bad idea. Miami has the highest incidence of AIDS in the US, according to a 2002 study. Fortunately, most of the bars, especially the gay ones, have big bowls full of free condoms for patrons to help themselves to.

Left **ATM** Center **Sign for mail** Right **Phonecard**

TOP 10 Money and Communication Tips

1 Exchanging Money

Except for American Express, there are virtually no exchange places as such, but you can go into any bank to exchange money. All in all, however, it's best to avoid this ritual (see below).

2 Automated Teller Machines

This is the most sensible way to get the cash you need. If you have an ATM card of any sort, chances are it will work in almost any machine and you will be able to draw cash out any time, up to your daily limit. There will be a fee, but the time and hassle you save is worth it. Don't forget your PIN!

3 Credit Cards

Doing anything in the US without a credit card is almost unthinkable, especially in a hotel.

4 Travelers' Checks

As a backup, travelers' checks can be useful, but these days they are outdated and almost pointless.

5 Banks

Banks are numerous and all have walk-up ATM machines handily located. If you must perform some sort of transaction inside, the hours are usually 9am–4pm, Monday to Thursday, and 9am–6pm Friday. Some banks are also open on Saturday mornings.

6 Sales Tax

Unlike in some countries, sales tax is not included in the marked price of anything, including restaurant meals. The only items sales tax is not added to are most groceries. Florida's sales tax at present is 6 percent, but local taxes can bump that up considerably. Hoteliers in Miami add on 12.5 percent to your bill.

7 Public Phones

You'll find these at gas stations, restaurants, hotels, on the sidewalk, and elsewhere. For long distance calls, it's easier to use a phonecard, which you can buy from any convenience store. Using your credit card is possible, too, but pricey. For making any call in Miami, even next door, you must dial the 305 area code, but not the 1 before it.

8 Cell Phones

If your cell phone (mobile) is not compatible with US networks, then renting a cell phone to use while here is a sensible option. You'll find vendors at the airport upon arrival.

9 Postal Services

Post offices are usually open from 9am–5pm on weekdays, with some open on Saturday mornings, too. Stamps are sold in many drugstores, hotels, and grocery stores. All domestic mail goes first class, and you should use airmail for any overseas mail. If you want it to get there the next day in the US, go for Express Mail.

10 Fax and Internet Access

Internet cafés abound. Many hotels, and especially hostels, offer the service, too, usually for a charge. A good central Internet point in South Beach, just a block from the sand, is Devine Lounge. It's also a lounge and a decent restaurant where a certain amount of people-watching goes on – after all, it's SoBe!

Directory

American Express
330 Biscayne Blvd., Downtown • 305-358-7350 • 9–5:30 Mon–Fri, 9–5 Sat

Lost Credit Cards
VISA 1-800-336-8472 • MasterCard 1-800-843-0777 • American Express 1-800-528-4800 • Discover 1-800-347-2683 • Diners Club, 1-800-234-6377

Lost Travelers' Checks
American Express 1-800-221-7282 • Thomas Cook 1-800-223-7373.

Devine Lounge
910 Collins Ave • 305-534-1414

Unusually, the Miami 305 phone code must be dialled even when in the city, so remember to use it when making calls.

Streetsmart

Left **Center for tourist information** Center **Cheap eats** Right **Bicycling**

Ways to Save Money

1 Fly-Drive Packages

To get the most out of Miami, you need a car. Some of the fly-drive packages can save a great deal of money.

2 Off-Season

There's no doubt that visiting the area out of season costs much, much less. Hotel prices can be reduced by up to two-thirds. It's true that the weather is a lot muggier, but the ocean breezes make beach life tolerable, and everything else is air-conditioned. Also ask your travel agent or check the web for promotional fares, but be sure to get all the details.

3 Discount Booklets

Coupon brochures – often with useful maps – are available free at most tourist stops or information desks. Savings can often be significant if you've got a large group or family to pay for. There are sometimes accommodations and tour discount coupons, too.

4 Free Sights

Not much is free here, apart from the stupendous beaches. But there are parks and gardens that charge no admission, and strolling around the busy streets doesn't have to involve any outlay. One of the greatest pleasures is watching the ships go by, either from the bottom of Miami Beach, at South Pointe, or from Mallory Square in Key West.

5 Saving Money on Accommodations

It's always worth trying to bargain the price down a bit, since no rates are cast in concrete. You can get an especially good deal in many places if you negotiate a weekly rate. If you're traveling on business of any kind, you can also request a commercial rate.

6 Cheap Eats

Although there are many very expensive restaurants, there are many more chain fast-food franchises. If such fare disagrees with your palate, you'll also find excellent local eateries that charge relatively little for good sandwiches. Otherwise, restaurants and bars often supply free food during cocktail hour, if you order a drink. Some restaurants also offer early bird specials for patrons dining between 5pm and 6pm.

7 Picnicking

You can have your picnic anywhere that there isn't a sign forbidding it. Many public parks and all state parks have tables and other facilities and you can take your snack to the beach with you, too. However, be aware that littering in the US is severely frowned upon, so dispose of all refuse in the bins provided.

8 Pay in Cash

Often when making a purchase of any kind, especially in a shop, you can negotiate a discount if you pay in cash, rather than by credit card. The shopkeeper will be saving the charge from the credit card company and willing to pass on some of that saving – usually 2–5 percent – to you.

9 Bicycling

Not only is it healthier, allowing you to work on your tan and breathe in the energy-charged air here, but it's also one of the very best ways to get around most of the prime areas in South Florida. Biking around South Beach, Key Biscayne, Key West, and even along certain trails in the Everglades is, for many, the only way to go, and the money you can save is significant.

10 Shop Wisely

Whatever you're in the market for, from tickets to trinkets, take the time to do a little research and price-comparison. Chances are you can find the same or similar item for much less if you shop around. If it's a toiletry need, for example, head for one of the large, all-purpose drugstores, where there are generic brands of almost everything, from contact lens solution to mouthwash, usually at half the name-brand price.

Left **Disabled sign** Right **"Kneeling" bus**

Senior and Disabled Travelers

1 Retirees
For decades, all of Florida has been retirement heaven – or "God's Waiting-Room," as it's sometimes not so graciously called. Hence, there are many facilities for senior citizens.

2 Senior Travelers
Traveling in South Florida is relatively easy for seniors, and there are good programs to allow seniors to get the most out of their experience here. Contact Elderhostel.

3 Tips for Seniors
Take advantage of the extra time you've earned, allowing yourself to get to know Miami in greater depth than the fly-by tourist. Use the cooler modes of getting around – on South Beach the air-conditioned South Beach Local, and on Key West the shaded and breezy Conch Tour Train.

4 Resources for Seniors
Membership in the American Association of Retired Persons is open to US and Canadian residents age 50 or over. They provide up-dated travel information and discounts. Elderhostel is for people 60 and over.

5 Discounts and Freebies
Senior citizens are eligible for discounts on travel, car rental, accommodations,

museum entrance, and more. Take your ID. Sometimes the definition of "senior" can be as young as 55! If you're a US citizen or permanent resident, get a Golden Age Passport, which entitles you to free entry into all national parks, monuments, and historic sites.

6 Disabled Travelers
Generally speaking, the area is well-set-up for disabled travelers. Mobility International USA and the Society for the Advancement of Travelers with Handicaps (SATH) have more information.

7 Accessibility to Buildings
All public buildings in the US are required by law to provide wheelchair access. However, older Deco hotels and many of the old guesthouses might have only one disabled-accessible room.

8 Transportation
Public buses "kneel," and the other public forms of transportation also have wheelchair access. Some taxis and car rental companies have special equipment: ask in advance.

9 Tips for the Disabled
For getting around such areas as South Beach or Key West, take full advantage of electrically powered transport, either

your own wheelchair or a rented one. The heat and humidity can make exertion uncomfortable.

10 Resources for the Disabled
Check out Access-Able, Directions Unlimited, and Wheels Up! on the Internet. Also call Miami-Dade Disability Services and the Miami Lighthouse for the Blind.

Directory

Miami-Dade Elder Help Line
305-670-4357

The American Association of Retired Persons
1-888-687-2277

Elderhostel
1-877-426-8056

Mobility Websites
- www.miusa.org
- www.sath.org
- www.access-able.com
- www.wheelsup.com

Miami-Dade Disability Services and Independent Living
305-547-5444

SATH (Travelers with Handicaps)
212-447-7284

Miami Lighthouse for the Blind
305-856-2288

The Access Hotline
305-358-4357

Left **Local cops** Center **Turtle – look out for injured wildlife** Right **Gay nightclubbers**

Hotlines and Helplines

Directory

Switchboard of Miami
305-358-4357

Miami Time & Weather
305-324-8811

Fish & Wildlife Commission
305-956-2500
305-526-2789

Poison Control
1-800-282-3171

Gay Anti-Violence Hotline
305-358-4357.

First Call for Help/Crisis Line
305-358-4357

The Teen Link Line
305-377-8336, for tapes, 305-377-8255 to speak to a counselor

Florida Kid Care
1-888-540-5437

Runaway Hotline (Miami Bridge)
305-635-8953

Teach More, Love More (24 hours)
305-631-8111

Rape Hotline
305-585-7273

Rape Treatment Center:
305-585-5185

Miami-Dade Central Intake and Detoxification
305-638-6540

Miami-Dade Advocates for Victims
305-758-2546

1 General Medical and Police

The all-purpose number for any emergency is 911. For less urgent situations, use the phone numbers for the hotlines and helplines listed here.

8 General Helpline

The 24-hour Switchboard of Miami can help with information about local services.

9 Miami Time and Weather

If you're planning an outdoor activity of any sort, you can look in the newspaper or online to see the weather forecast. The best way to get the most current report on weather conditions and probabilities is to the call the special number for the Greater Miami area.

10 Injured Wildlife

In your outdoor exploration of South Florida, particularly on the beaches, waterways, or in the Everglades, you may encounter injured animals or birds, large or small. You can call the Fish and Wildlife Commission to get help for them.

2 Poison Help-line

The poison control helpline gives quick advice on antidotes and how to handle any crisis related to poisoning, including food poisoning and allergic reactions.

3 Gay Anti-Violence

The Gay Anti-Violence Hotline offers support and referral services to gay and bisexual victims of harassment, domestic violence, sexual assault, and hate crimes that occur anywhere in the Greater Miami Area.

4 Psychological Crisis Line

Miami provides a First Call for Help/Crisis Line, which is like a 911 line for psychological or emotional problems and dilemmas.

5 Help for Parents and Children

The Teen Link Line aims to provide "Straight Up Information on Stuff that Matters" to teens, with 80 taped informational messages on topics of concern to adolescents and links to counselors. There are also numbers for the Florida Kid Care line (toll free), Runaway Hotline, and the Teach More, Love More line.

6 Rape Crisis Lines

Counseling is provided for any sort of trauma relating to sexuality and sexual abuse.

7 Drug and Alcohol Counseling

The Miami-Dade Central Intake and Detoxification Center is geared up to take calls from anyone suffering from substance abuse problems.

Left **Hotel lobby** Center **Motel** Right **Parking lot**

TOP 10 Accommodation Tips

1 Area Options
Every sort of accommodation is available in South Florida, from a simple dorm bed in a hostel in a villa in an unbelievably luxurious resort on its own island. Most of the hotels, motels, and the like are on or near the beach, or at least some body of water. Inland, good choices might put you in an interesting and colorfully ethnic urban area, or in a quaint old Everglades town.

2 Needs and Desires
The best way to decide what suits you best is to read up on this fascinatingly rich destination. If it's the outdoors and sports you're after, head directly for the Keys. If it's world-class nightlife, the choice is South Beach.

3 Price Range
The price range is vast. Even on South Beach in high season, just two blocks from the beach, you can find a room for two, with private bath, for as little as $25 per person per night. Or, a block away, a penthouse suite in some fabulous Deco landmark is up for $2,500.

4 Special Deals
Be aware that many hotels have a minimum stay requirement, but often offer a good deal if you book by the week.

5 Making Reservations
If you want to go for the bargain accommodations in high season, it's crucial that you book as early as you possibly can. Make sure the reservation is solid by guaranteeing it with a credit card, and doubly confirming it by way of both fax and email. If you're expecting to arrive late, find out the latest acceptable arrival time before your reservation is subject to cancellation.

6 Without Reservations
Trying to find something on the spot from December to April is not recommended, at least not in South Beach or Key West, especially on weekends. It might take a long time to find, and you run the risk of having to pay even more than top dollar. Taking pot luck is only a good idea in low season.

7 Tipping
The usual practice is to tip the bellboy $1 per bag, both when he brings your luggage to your room and when you depart. If you leave your luggage in storage, the tip should be the same. If your hotel has valet parking, you should tip the guy $2 or so each time he delivers your car to you. If you enjoyed their service, you can also tip the front desk staff and concierge whatever feels right.

8 Hidden Extras
There can be many of these, so get it all clear from the start. If there's valet parking, that can cost about $15–20 per day. Phone calls made from your room phone generally start at 50 cents each, and can be charged on a per-minute basis in some cases. Finally, when you check out, you will notice a rather hefty hotel tax of at least 10 percent has been added on, depending on where the hotel is in South Florida.

9 Traveling with Kids
Family travel is the bread-and-butter of South Florida tourism, and every major hotel or resort offers a wide range of activities and services – supervised play areas, baby-sitting, special games, coloring books, etc. Usually children under a certain age (sometimes as high as 18) can stay free in their parents' room. In addition, many restaurants offer kids' meals at reduced prices.

10 Parking
Valet parking is convenient, but often terribly expensive, and it's impossible to keep the 24-hour meters fed. The only sensible option is to put your car in a parking garage, where you can get a more reasonable rate, and leave it.

Left **Biltmore Hotel** Center **The Breakers** Right **Wyndham Grand Bay Hotel**

TOP 10 Hotels: The Lap of Luxury

1 Loews
SoBe's biggest Deco tower, newly built, is located on a sandy beach in the heart of it all. The multifaceted property incorporates an old hotel – the rebuilt St. Moritz – six restaurants and a beautiful, mosaic-tile, oceanfront swimming pool. ✆ *1601 Collins Ave, South Beach • Map S3 • 1-800-235-6397• www. loewshotels.com • $$$$$*

2 Mandarin Oriental
Located on Brickell Key (Claughton Island), near the Port of Miami and Downtown. The curved building means rooms have a water view. Check the website for special rates. ✆ *500 Brickell Key Dr • Map P3 • 305-913-8288 • www.mandarin oriental.com • $$$$$*

3 Sheraton Bal Harbour Resort
It's a 10-acre (4-ha) tropical garden with a "mystic" rope bridge suspended over a lagoon and close proximity to Bal Harbour. These and other features have drawn the likes of the Clintons and Bill Gates to stay at this high-end paradise. ✆ *9701 Collins Ave, Bal Harbour • Map H2 • 1-800-999-9898 • www. sheratonhotels.com • $$$$$*

4 Hotel Interconti-nental Miami
In the heart of the business district, this is Downtown's finest, with spectacular views and gourmet dining. A huge Henry Moore sculpture adorns the lobby; the comfortable, quiet rooms sport marble bathrooms. ✆ *100 Chopin Plaza, at Biscayne Blvd • Map P2 • 1-800-327-3005 • www. ichotelsgroup.com • $$$$*

5 Biltmore Hotel
A beautiful landmark structure *(see p18)* with the splendor and glamour of a by-gone era and epicurean pleasures, too, in the Palme d'Or restaurant. Rooms are in the grand European tradition, and you can swim in one of the world's largest hotel pools. ✆ *1200 Anastasia, Coral Gables • 800-727-1926 • www. biltmorehotel.com • $$$$$*

6 Wyndham Grand Bay Hotel
Of stepped construction like some Aztec temple, and loaded with luxuries, such as Persian carpets, Chinese porcelains, crystal chandeliers, designer furniture, and original art. Luciano Pavarotti has a suite here. ✆ *2669 Bayshore Dr, Coconut Grove • Map G3 • 1-800-996-3426 • www.wyndham.com • $$$*

7 Mayfair House
Set on top of an exclusive shopping mall, the hotel's large suites have rich mahogany furniture, marble baths, and balconies. The style is a mix of Spain and the Far East, enhanced by Art Nouveau touches.✆ *3000 Florida Ave, Coconut Grove • Map G3 • 1-800-433-4555 • www.mayfairhousehotel. com • $$$$*

8 Four Seasons (Palm Beach)
Possibly the finest service you'll ever experience, from fresh fruit and orchids in your large room with sea view, to a towncar shuttle to and from downtown Palm Beach, and one of the best restaurants around. ✆ *Lake Worth • Map D2 • 1-800-432-2335 • www. fourseasons.com • $$$$$*

9 The Breakers (Palm Beach)
A Palm Beach landmark of the Gilded-Age tradition, whose décor evokes the Spanish Revival taste that Flagler brought to Florida in the 1890s. Modern comforts are epitomized by the spa annex. ✆ *1 South County Rd • Map D2 • 888-273-2537 • www. thebreakers.com • $$$$$*

10 Pier House & Caribbean Spa (Key West)
In the heart of the historic Seaport District, the hotel is surrounded by lush tropical gardens. It has four unique bars, three award-winning restaurants, and luxurious Island-colonial style rooms, all with ocean, pool, or garden views. ✆ *One Duval Street, Key West • Map A6 • 1-800-327-8340 • www. pierhouse.com • $$$$$*

On pp146–53 are hotel listings for Miami, Fort Lauderdale, Palm Beach, and the Keys. For more hotels outside Miami See p131

Price Categories

For a standard, double room per night (with breakfast if included), taxes, and extra charges.

$	under $100
$$	$100–$200
$$$	$200–$250
$$$$	$250–$300
$$$$$	over $300

Left **Delano** Right **Raleigh**

TOP 10 SoBe Deco-Dence

1 Tides
This fully restored Art Deco landmark hotel, with its distinctive coral rock entrance, is in the heart of all the SoBe attractions. The decor is epitomized by cool, white linen and overstuffed sofas and easy chairs in all rooms. Superb service. ⍟ *1220 Ocean Drive • Map S3 • 305-604-5070 • www.tidessouth beach.com • $$$$$*

2 Delano
A very trippy and ultra-luxurious Post-Modern wonder. The original, rather austere white exterior has been restored without any fuss. But inside, the divine madness of Philippe Starke, along with hilarious Dali- and Gaudi-inspired designs have been given room to play. The very chi-chi and daring Blue Door restaurant is co-owned by Madonna. ⍟ *1685 Collins Ave • Map S2 • 305-672-2000 • www.morgans hotelgroup.com • $$$$$*

3 Raleigh
On the pricey side, to be sure, but nothing less than fabulous. The décor has endless style and panache, often with period pieces. The eye-popping swimming pool is immortalized in several Esther Williams movies. ⍟ *1775 Collins Ave • Map S2 • 1-800-848-1775 • ww.raleighhotel. com • $$$$*

4 The Hotel of South Beach
"Tiffany," as proclaimed by the neon tower, was The Hotel's name until the famous jewelry company sued. It is so long on style and comfort, designed by Todd Oldham, that it qualifies as a work of art in itself. ⍟ *801 Collins Ave • Map R4 • 1-877-843-4683 • www.thehotelofsouth beach.com • $$$*

5 Nash
One of the more sober Deco edifices, built in 1938 and impeccably restored with every comfort. The rooms are done in a tastefully subdued Post-Modern style by noted designer Peter Page, who also restored other South Beach landmarks. ⍟ *1120 Collins Ave • Map S4 • 305-674-7800 • www. hotelnash.com • $$*

6 Avalon
Actually two hotels on opposite corners of 7th Street, these perfectly located Deco bon-bons are excellent value. You're in the middle of SoBe's most popular stretch, and you get comfortable rooms and a complimentary continental breakfast. ⍟ *700 Ocean Drive • Map S4 • 1-800-933-3306 • www.avalon hotel.com • $$$*

7 Albion
Excellent value, considering the extreme chic that exudes from the cutting-edge restoration of this great Deco original. Check out the pool's peek-a-boo portholes. ⍟ *1650 James Ave at Lincoln Rd • Map S2 • 305-913-1000 • www.rubell hotels.com • $$*

8 National Hotel
Newly renovated Art Deco hotel in the right location to see and be seen, this is one of the coolest places on South Beach. It has one of the longest pools in Florida. ⍟ *1677 Collins Ave • Map S2 • 305-532-2311 • www. nationalhotel.com • $$$$*

9 Best Western South Beach
You can't say much for the name, but the property is actually four '30s Art Deco sugar cubes (the Kenmore, Taft, Bel Aire, and Davis) spread over the entire block between 10th and 11th Streets. All are freshly restored and set amid spacious gardens. ⍟ *1050 Washington Ave • Map R4 • 305-674-1930 • www.best western.com • $$*

10 Casa Grande Suite Hotel
This luxurious small hotel is one of the finest in the trendy South Beach area. Just step right out into all the nightlife. Newly renovated suites have amenities galore, including kitchens. ⍟ *834 Ocean Drive • Map S4 • 305-672-7003 • www.casagrande suitehotel.com • $$$$$*

For more on SoBe's Art Deco landmarks See pp10–13

Left **Ritz Carlton Hotel, Key Biscayne** Right **Boca Raton Resort**

🔟 Resorts and Spas

1 The Fisher Island Club

The billionaires who favor this very private island love the exclusivity that its remoteness provides. Personal golf-carts, quiet as a whisper, let you toodle around the many beaches, restaurants, clubs, etc. 🚫 Fisher Island Dr (off the MacArthur Causeway – free car ferry every 15 mins) • Map H3 • 1-800-537-3708 • $$$$$

2 Fontainebleau Resort & Towers, Miami Beach

One of the great Miami Beach hotels, built in the '50s. The restoration is now complete, and the effect is stunning. Rooms are large, and there is a huge beachside spa. 🚫 4441 Collins Ave • Map H3 • 1-800-548-8886 • www. fontainebleau.com • $$$$

3 Ritz Carlton, Key Biscayne

Located in the exclusive Grand Bay community of Key Biscayne, this is a grand hotel in every respect. Beautiful interiors, two pools, tennis courts, a spa, and a hotel restaurant rated in the country's top 50. 🚫 455 Grand Bay Drive, Key Biscayne • Map H4 • 305-365-4500 • www.ritz carlton.com • $$$$$

4 Trump International Sonesta Beach Resort

Right on the ocean this 32-floor, lushly

landscaped hotel has many amenities on offer, including a spa, a host of programs for kids, a 24-hour exercise facility, and a business center. 🚫 18001 Collins Ave, Sunny Isles • Map H3 • 305-692-5500 • www.trumpsonesta. com • $$$$$

5 Fairmont Turnberry Isle, Aventura

Very grand, with oriental carpets, marble accents, and hundreds of acres of landscaped islands and waterways, a golf course, tennis courts, spa, private beach, and harbor. The feeling is welcoming, clubby, and very rich. 🚫 19999 W Country Club Dr, Aventura • Map H1 • 1-800-327-7028 • www.fairmont. com • $$$$$

6 Doral Golf Resort and Spa, Miami

Internationally famous for its championship golf course. In fact, there are seven golf courses, along with 15 tennis courts, water park, health club, and a world-class spa. 🚫 4400 NW 87th Ave, Miami • Map F3 • 1-800-713-6725 • www.doral resort.com • $$$$$

7 Boca Raton Resort and Club

The original buildings were built by one of Florida's early visionaries, Addison Mizner, in 1926. The mix of Mediterranean styles has been carried through, and opulent, fabled luxury is every-

where, down to the marble bathrooms with original polished brass fittings. 🚫 501 East Camino Real, Boca Raton • Map D3 • (561)-395-3000 • www. bocaresort.com • $$$$$

8 Cheeca Lodge, Islamorada

An amazing tropical island world, with a wonderful beach, various pools, golf, tennis, nature walks, hot-tubbing, sport fishing, snorkeling, windsurfing, etc. 🚫 Mile Marker 82, Islamorada • Map C5 • 305-664-4651 • www.cheeca.com • $$$$

9 Hawk's Cay Resort, Duck Key

Exclusive Keys resort offering dolphin encounters, fishing, an offshore sailing school, scuba diving, snorkeling, parasailing, kayaking, waterskiing, glass-bottom boat tours, and many other activities. 🚫 Mile Marker 61 • Map B6 • 305-743-7000 • www.hawkscay.com • $$$$$

10 Casa Marina Resort, Key West

Key West's first grand hotel still shows its posh roots. There is an air of reverie contrasting with the rest of the hectic island. Opulent public areas lead to understated rooms, many with water views. 🚫 1500 Reynolds St, Key West • Map A6 • 1-800-626-0777 • www. casamarinakeywest.com • $$$$$

Note: Unless otherwise stated, all hotels accept credit cards, have disabled access, private bathrooms, and air conditioning

Shelborne Resort

Price Categories

For a standard, double room per night (with breakfast if included), taxes, and extra charges.

$	under $100
$$	$100–$200
$$$	$200–$250
$$$$	$250–$300
$$$$$	over $300

TOP 10 Surfside Retreats

1 Shelborne Resort, South Beach

Directly on the Atlantic in the heart of South Beach, this Art Deco high-rise hotel is newly restored and once again quite elegant, its surprising affordability notwithstanding. The best feature is the stylish pool. ✆ 1801 Collins Ave • Map S2 • 1-800-327-8757 • www. shelborne.com • $$$$

2 Ritz Carlton, South Beach

Located in the historic Art Deco district, in a 1953 Morris Lapidus-designed landmark building. Just steps away from Lincoln Road dining and shopping and with 80 poolside rooms and 40 beach suites. ✆ 1 Lincoln Rd, Miami Beach • Map S2 • 786-276-4000 • www.ritz carlton.com • $$$$$

3 Betsy Ross Hotel, South Beach

The colonial-style hotel may seem incongruous on South Beach, but it was actually built at the same time as its Deco siblings: it just took a different fantasy turn. ✆ 1440 Ocean Drive • Map S3 • 305-531-3934 • www. betsyrosshotel.com • $$

4 Ocean Surf Hotel, Miami Beach

Well north of South Beach, this appealing 1940 Nautical-Deco boutique hotel is right on the ocean. Restored in 1997, the well-equipped rooms offer mini-fridges, safes, and cable TV. Continental breakfast is included. ✆ 7436 Ocean Terrace • Map H2 • 1-800-555-0411, 305-866-1648 • www.oceansurf.com • $$

5 Lago Mar, Fort Lauderdale

Lush tropical luxury right on its own flawless beach, with two pools, tennis courts, shuffleboard, and a complete spa. Rooms are very large, most with great views. Superb restaurants featuring exceptional Italian cuisine at Acquario and Black Angus steaks at Chops. Very popular with families – book well in advance. ✆ 1700 S. Ocean Lane • Map D3 • 1-800-524-6627 • $$$$

6 Windjammer Resort and Beach Club, Lauderdale-by-the-Sea

Two buildings with multi-level walkways and decks and two heated pools, plus gardens, all combine to give that special resort feel. Every unit is a complete apartment in itself. ✆ 4244 El Mar Drive • Map D3 • 954-776-4232 • www.windjammerbeach resort.com • $$

7 Kona Kai Resort, Key Largo

This is a truly magical hideaway, with lovely gardens. Each guestroom is uniquely decorated in refreshing Island style, using tropical fabrics, original art, and elegant simplicity. Private beach, pool, and Jacuzzi. ✆ 97802 Overseas Hwy • Map D3 • 1-800-365-7829 • www. konakairesort.com • $$$$

8 The Atlantic, Fort Lauderdale

This new luxury resort is in a great location. It is superbly furnished and has a spa, fitness center, and an award-winning chef, Don Petabono, at its Trina Restaurant. ✆ 601 N Fort Lauderdale Beach Blvd • Map D3 • 954-567-8020 • www.starwood. com/luxury • $$$$

9 Old Town Resorts, Key West

A marvelous collection of properties including the Southernmost Hotel, Southernmost on the Beach, La Mer House, and Dewey House. Each has its own character, but all have the charm to create oases of serenity within this buzzing island. ✆ 1319 Duval Street, Key West • Map A6 • 305-296-6577 • www.southern mostresorts.com • $$

10 Doubletree Grand Key Resort, Key West

The perfect place for families, or for those who want to have the choice – to party or not to party. Very close to excellent Smathers Beach. ✆ 3990 S. Roosevelt Blvd, Key West • Map A6 • 1-888-310-1540 • www.double treekeywest.com • $$$$

Left **South Beach Plaza Villas** Center **Hotel Place St. Michel** Right **Marquesa Hotel**

Guesthouse Charmers

1 South Beach Plaza Villas, SoBe

A true find in sometimes overdone SoBe. Very laid back and super-friendly, the place feels more like it's in the islands somewhere remote, yet you're just a block away from the beach intensity. The rooms have great character, and there's a tranquil garden to relax in. Book well in advance. ✆ 1411 Collins Ave • Map S3 • 305-531-1331 • www.south beachplazavillas.com • $$$$

2 Hotel Leon, SoBe

Unpretentious, understated, and above all comfortable, this period hotel (1929) has been warmly refurbished and is a cozy retreat with a European air. ✆ 841 Collins Ave • Map S4 • 305-673-3767 • www. hotelleon.com • $$$

3 Villa Paradiso Guesthouse, SoBe

All rooms have French doors that open onto the sunny courtyard and garden, and are nicely renovated and decorated with appealingly upholstered wrought iron furniture. Each accommodation has a full kitchen. ✆ 1415 Collins Ave • Map S3 • 305-532-0616 • www.villa paradisohotel.com • $$

4 Hotel Place St. Michel, Coral Gables

A European-style inn built in 1926, during the Merrick heyday (see p19).

Each room has its own unique personality, accented by carefully chosen antiques. ✆ 162 Alcazar Ave at Ponce de Leon Blvd • 1-800-848-4683 • www.hotelplacestmichel. com • $$

5 Sea Lord, Lauderdale-by-the-Sea

This small, charming resort is smack bang on the beach, but it is also close to shops and restaurants. The 48 rooms and suites have been recently renovated and most have a kitchen. ✆ 4140 Elmar Drive • Map D3 • 954-776-1505 • www.sealordhotel. com • $$

6 A Little Inn by the Sea, Lauderdale-by-the-Sea

Great value and loaded with charm, with its leafy courtyards and splashing fountains, right on the beach. Extras include free parking, bicycle use, chaises longues, tennis, barbecue, and a heated pool. ✆ 4546 El Mar Drive • Map D3 • 1-800-492-0311 • www.alittleinn.com • $$

7 Barnacle Bed & Breakfast, Big Pine Key

Tucked among towering palm trees on a white sandy beach, this is an intriguing Caribbean-style home where leisurely breezes prevail. Unique furnishings in each room. Breakfast is served in the atrium overlooking the

ocean. ✆ 1557 Long Beach Drive • Map B6 • 305-872-3298 • $$

8 The Gardens Hotel, Key West

In a serene, shaded world of botanical gardens, this plantation-style property is certainly Key West's grande dame among guesthouses. Five buildings comprise the hotel, including a Bahamian "eyebrow" cottage. All rooms have garden views and most have Jacuzzis. All in all, sumptuous. ✆ 526 Angela St • Map A6 • 1-800-526-2664 • www. gardenshotel.com • $$$$

9 Marquesa Hotel, Key West

Built in 1884, the extravagant compound of four exquisitely restored "conch" houses is now set amid lush greenery. All rooms and suites have marble bathrooms. ✆ 600 Fleming St • Map A6 • 1-800-869-4631 • www. marquesa.com • $$$$$

10 The Mermaid & the Alligator, Key West

One of Key West's very finest, a 1904 beauty, with colonial Caribbean décor and wonderful gardens. Rooms have period furnishings, and they feel private and deeply cozy. Full breakfast is served by the pool; wine in the afternoons. ✆ 726 Truman Ave • Map A6 • 1-800-726-1894 • www. kwmermaid.com • $$$

Note: Unless otherwise stated, all hotels accept credit cards, have disabled access, private bathrooms, and air conditioning

Price Categories

For a standard, double room per night (with breakfast if included), taxes, and extra charges.

$	under $100
$$	$100–$200
$$$	$200–$250
$$$$	$250–$300
$$$$$	over $300

Southwinds Motel

ᵀᴼᴾ10 Exceptional Value Places

1 Hotel Astor, SoBe
Stay just a couple of blocks away from the beach and get a top-quality 1936 Deco gem. Rooms are large and fully soundproofed, bathrooms have marble walls and floors, and the pool area has gardenia hedges and night-blooming jasmine. ◈ 956 Washington Ave • Map R4 • 1-800-270-4981 • www.hotelastor.com • $$

2 Cadet Hotel, SoBe
With its festive Deco façade wrapped around a corner, this little find has one of the most enviable locations in South Beach. Comfortable, rather stylish rooms, and very efficient service. Clark Gable once stayed here. ◈ 1701 James Ave • Map S2 • www.cadethotel.com • 1-800-432-2338 • $$

3 James Hotel, SoBe
From the moment you cross the threshold everywhere you look there are brightly painted tiles, murals, and all manner of whimsical touches, including at least five different "Welcome" signs. Make reservations in advance – the location is fantastic. ◈ 1680 James Ave • Map S2 • 305-531-1125 • $

4 Tide Vacation Apartments, Hollywood Beach
Facing the sea, directly on Hollywood Beach's Broadwalk, each accommodation is a spacious efficiency (self-catering) apartment. ◈ 2800 North Surf Rd, at Coolidge • Map D3 • 954-923-3864 • www.tideapartments.com • Limited dis acc • $$

5 Beachcomber, Pompano Beach
An extraordinarily exclusive feel at very reasonable prices. Accommodations range from villas, to rooms with or without kitchens, to penthouse suites. The distinctive wrap-around balconies add a plush touch to the architecture. ◈ 1200 S. Ocean Blvd • Map D3 • 954-941-7830 • www.beachcomberhotel.com • $$

6 Kon Tiki Resort, Islamorada
A real homey Olde Keys experience. Not at all stylish, in fact, just a little bit raw, but welcoming and comfortable. It has gardens, a sandy beach, a heated freshwater pool, a protected lagoon on Florida Bay, and a boat ramp. ◈ 81200 Overseas Hwy., Mile Marker 82 • Map C5 • 305-664-4702 • www.kontikiresort.com • $$

7 Duval House, Key West
These gracious Victorian twins and their white picket fence will win your heart. The rooms are accented with lots of wicker and florals, and everyone seems extraordinarily friendly. The location is unsurpassed for convenience. ◈ 815 Duval St • Map A6 • 1-800-223-8825 • www.duvalhousekeywest.com • $$$

8 Atlantic Shores Resort, Key West
Key West's only oceanfront adult alternative resort, catering to the most mixed clientele you can imagine. The biggest draw is the clothing-optional pool and sundeck right out on the Atlantic, which is pretty much "Party Central" most hours of the day and night. ◈ 510 South St • Map A6 • 305-296-2491 • www.atlanticshoresresort.com • Limited dis acc • $$

9 Abaco Inn, Key West
On a secluded lane in the lush heart of the Old Town district, not far from amenities. All rooms are smoke-free and decorated with warm, restful colors. Out back, there's a relaxing tropical garden. ◈ 415 Julia St • Map A6 • 1-800-358-6307 • www.abaco-inn.com • $$

10 Southwind Motel, Key West
An old-fashioned, unpretentious motel. There's a large freshwater pool and sundeck, set in a tropical garden. Some rooms have kitchenettes, and all guests have off-street parking. ◈ 1321 Simonton St • Map A6 • 305-296-2215 • www.keywestsouthwind.com • $$

Left **Clay Hotel and Youth Hostel** Right **Peter Miller Hotel**

Hostels and Budget

1 Clay Hotel and Youth Hostel, SoBe

This enchanting Spanish-style place, built in 1925 and beautifully refurbished, also happens to be the biggest bargain in the Western World and is always teeming with international youth. Book very far in advance to get a place. ⊗ *1438 Washington Avenue, South Beach • Map S3 • 305-534-2988 • www.clayhotel.com • $*

2 Floyd's Youth Hostel, Fort Lauderdale

A hostel with a friendly, relaxing atmosphere. There are four beds per room and all apartment units have two bedrooms. Some private rooms are available. If you prefer a seaside location, ask about their beach hostel. ⊗ *445 SE 16th St, Fort Lauderdale • Map D3 • 954-462-0631 • www.floydshostel.com • $*

3 Miami Beach Travelers' Hostel

One of the cheapest places right in the middle of the SoBe action, this hostel radiates a fun-loving atmosphere of camaraderie, even though it is a bit grotty. Amenities include internet, kitchen, and laundry. ⊗ *236 9th St, South Beach • Map R4 • 1-800-978-6787 • www.sobehostel.com • $*

4 Tropics Hotel and Hostel, SoBe

This is a genuine Art Deco building, complete with neon marquee, in one of the most desirable locations on South Beach. It's clean and comfortable and, given the location, worth two to three times the asking price. There's even a pool. Book in advance. ⊗ *1550 Collins Ave, South Beach • Map S3 • 305-531-0361 • www.tropicshotel.com • $*

5 Peter Miller Hotel, SoBe

Authentic 1935 Deco, although a bit down-at-the-heel, this place promotes itself as "the best deal on South Beach" – the rates are extremely good if you negotiate for a week or so. Rooms are large and comfortable. Tends toward an older clientele. ⊗ *1900 Collins Ave, South Beach • Map S2 • 305-531-7611 • $*

6 Berkeley Shore Hotel, SoBe

Definitely one of the coolest Deco buildings around, with its elaborate façade, and riot of Island-style color inside. The proprietors and staff are mostly Cubans – there's a vivacity about the place that feels Caribbean. Rooms are spacious, though basic. Many have kitchenettes. ⊗ *1610 Collins Ave, South Beach • Map S3 • 305-531-5731 • $*

7 Green Island Inn, Fort Lauderdale

An amazing deal. The whole ambience is so inviting and spacious it feels like a resort. Homey touches are everywhere, and each room has its own uniquely tropical look, as well as a full kitchen. Book well in advance. ⊗ *3300 NE 27th St, Fort Lauderdale Beach • Map D3 • 954-566-8951 • www.greenislandinn.com • $*

8 Florida Beach Hostel, Fort Lauderdale

A clean and fresh place near the beach, with a nice rooftop patio and tropical garden courtyard for picnicking. There's free parking and some free food. ⊗ *2115 N. Ocean Blvd, Fort Lauderdale • Map D3 • 954-567-7275 • www.fortlauderdalehostel.com • $*

9 Budget Key West

No pool, no lobby, no frills, but it's clean, comfortable, bright, secure, within easy walking distance of most places in Old Town, and the vernacular architecture is appealing. All rooms have a kitchenette. ⊗ *1031 Eaton St, Key West • Map A6 • 1-800-403-2866 • www.budgetkeywest.com • $$*

10 Key West Youth Hostel

Offers snorkeling trips and scuba instruction, plus bike rentals. It has a courtyard, picnic area, and game rooms, but only 10 private rooms, so book in advance. ⊗ *718 South St, Key West • Map A6 • 305-296-5719 • www.keywesthostel.com • $*

Note: Unless otherwise stated, all hotels accept credit cards, have disabled access, private bathrooms, and air conditioning

Royal Palms Resort

Price Categories

For a standard, double room per night (with breakfast if included), taxes, and extra charges.	**$** under $100
	$$ $100–$200
	$$$ $200–$250
	$$$$ $250–$300
	$$$$$ over $300

🔟 Gay and Lesbian Hotels

1 Island House, South Beach and Haulover Beach

Two properties for gay males, with a wide variety of room configurations available in both places at very reasonable rates. ® *1428 Collins Ave, South Beach / 715 82nd St at Harding Ave, Surfside, Haulover Beach • Map S3 • 1-800-382-2422 for both • www.islandhousesouth beach.com • Some rooms have shared bathrooms • $*

2 Sobe You, SoBe

In a quiet neighborhood, five blocks from the beach, is one of the best gay and lesbian guesthouses in Miami. Attractions include a sun deck, pool, wine-and-cheese parties, and a gourmet breakfast by the pool. ® *1018 Jefferson Ave at 10th St, South Beach • Map R4 • 1-877-599-5247 • www.sobeyou.us • $$*

3 Hotel St. Augustine, Miami Beach

This small, chic boutique hotel is stylish and gay-friendly. All rooms have a steam shower and a console full of hand-made soaps, lotions, massage oils, and even candles. ® *347 Washington Ave, Miami Beach • Map R5 • 305-532-0570 • www. hotelstaugustine.com • $$*

4 Pineapple Point, Fort Lauderdale

Fort Lauderdale's premier accommodation for gay men is like a tropical rain forest, complete with orchids and a clothing-optional pool. Every comfort has been seen to. ® *315 NE 16 Terrace, Fort Lauderdale • Map D3 • 1-888-844-7295 • www. pineapplepoint.com • $$$$*

5 The Flamingo, Fort Lauderdale

A thoroughly pleasant place for gay men only, just two blocks from the beach. The interior exudes an understated colonial charm, with fountains, manicured gardens, a clothing-optional pool, four-poster beds, and white-on-white bedding. ® *2727 Terramar St, Fort Lauderdale • Map D3 • 1-800-283-4786 • www.the flamingoresort.com • $$$*

6 Royal Palms Resort, Fort Lauderdale

Gay men only are catered to here, in a lush tropical setting with clothing-optional pool. Rooms and suites have two-line phones, CD-players, high-speed internet access. ® *2901 Terramar, Fort Lauderdale Beach • Map D3 • 1-800-237-7256 • www. royalpalms.com • $$$$*

7 Island House for Men, Key West

For gay men only, this beautiful property is clothing-optional and very cruisy, featuring a poolside café, sauna and steam room, bar, gym, and erotic video lounge. ® *1129 Fleming St, Key West • Map A6 • 1-800-890-6284 • www.island housekeywest.com • $$*

8 Coral Tree Inn and Oasis Guest-house, Key West

The award-winning male-only duo, on opposite sides of Fleming St, form the largest accommoda-tion option on a very gay block. All properties along here are beautifully re-stored period buildings with heated pools, Jacuzzis, and all the local charm. ® *822 & 823 Fleming St, Key West • Map A6 • 1-800-362-7477 • www.keywest-allmale. com • $$*

9 Lighthouse Court Guesthouse Resort, Key West

Another clothing-optional, gay-males-only resort comprising 10 restored houses a block off Duval Street. ® *902 Whitehead St, Key West • Map A6 • 305-294-9588 • www.light housecourt.com • $$*

10 Pearl's Rainbow, Key West

Key West's only women-only guesthouse, well located just two blocks from the beach. You'll find extensive shady and sunny decks, two pools, two hot tubs, and Pearl's Patio, a poolside bar. Continental breakfast is included. ® *525 United St, Key West • Map A6 • 1-800-749-6696 • www. pearlsrainbow.com • $$*

Index

Page numbers in **bold** type refer to main entries

A

A & B Lobster House 125
Abaco Inn (Key West) 151
Accommodations 131, 145
    see also hotels
Addict 94
Agustin Gainza Gallery 85, 88
Ah-Tah-Thi-Ki and Billie Swamp 29
Ah-Tah-Thi-Ki **29**, 41
AIDS Memorial (Key West) 123
Airport information 135
Albion 147
Alfajores 61
Alhambra Water Tower (Coral Gables) 48
Alice's at La-Te-Da (Key West) 130
Americanoom (Chryssa) 21
Ancient Spanish Monastery 91
Andiamo! 95
Anhinga and Gumbo Limbo Trails 29
Anis, Albert 13
Annual Conch-blowing Contest 121
Anokha Fine Indian Cuisine 105
Anthropologie (Miami Beach) 75
Aqua Night Club 123
Arch Creek Park and Museum 93
Archeo 122
Architectural walk 83–6
Architectural Wonders 46–7
Around Miami and the Keys 70–131
Art By God 94
Art Deco District Welcome Center 75
Art Galleries
    Agustin Gainza Gallery 85, 88
    Ambrosino Gallery 43
    ArtSouth 110
    Artspace/Virginia Miller Gallery 43
    Barbara Gillman Gallery 43
    Bernice Steinbaum Gallery 43
    Fredric Snitzer Gallery 43
    Gallery at the Kona Kai Resort 122
    Kevin Bruk Gallery 43
    Locust Projects 43
    Margulies Collection 43
    Midori Gallery 101, 104
    Modernism Gallery 104
    Rubell Family Collection 43
Art of Shaving, The 94
Atabey 110
Atalantic, The (Fort Lauderdale) 149
Atlantic Shores Resort (Key West) 123, 151

Atlantis Condominium 46
Audubon House and Tropical Gardens (Key West) 27
Audubon, John James 27
Avalon 147
Aviary, The 110
Awful Arthur's 125

B

B.E.D 77
Bahama Village (Key West) 26
Bahia Honda State Park **31**, 117, 118
Bal Harbour 92
Balans 76
Baleen 105
Bank of America Tower 46, 84
Barbacle Bed & Breakfast (Big Pine Key) 150
Barbara Capitman 13, 45
Barnacle Historic State Park 100–101, 103
Barnes & Noble Booksellers 101, 104
Bartless, Frederic and Evelyn 25
Barton G – The Restaurant 79
Basketball 35
Bayfront Park 83, 86
Bayside Marketplace 50, 56, **83**, 86
Beachcomber (Pompano Beach) 151
Beach Patrol Stations 11
Beach Resorts 30–31
Beacon Hotel 10, 147
Berkeley Shore Hotel (SoBe) 152
Berlin's Cigar and Cocktail Bar 124
Best Western South Beach 147
Betsy Ross Hotel (SoBe) 149
Bice 95
Big Cypress Swamp 28
Bill Baggs Cape Florida 31, 72–3
Billie Swamp Safari Wildlife Park (Everglades) **29**, 41, 131
Biltmore Hotel **18**, 46, 99, 146
Biscayne National Underwater Park 108
Bishop O'Connell 49
Bistro Mezzaluna 24
Black beans and rice 61
Black Grove 103
Blackened grouper 61
Blue Club 77
Boardwalk (Fort Lauderdale) 53
Boca Raton Resort and Club 148
Bongos Cuban Café 58, 77
Bonnet House (Fort Lauderdale) 25
Books & Books 18, 51, 102, 104
Books and Books (Miami Beach) 75
Botánica El Aguila Vidente **15**, 85, 88
Bourbon Street Complex (Key West) 123
Boy Bar 76

Breakers (Palm Beach) 146
Breakwater Hotel **11**
Brickell, William 45
Brigade 2506 Memorial 85
Brigham Gardens (SoBe) 150
Broadwalk (Fort Lauderdale) 24
Broward, Governor N.B. 45
Buck 15 Lounge 76
Budget Key West 152
Buffett, Jimmy 27
Bull, The 124

C

Cadet Hotel (SoBe) 151
Café Cubano 61
Café Protegé (West Palm Beach) 130
Café Tu Tu Tango (Coconut Grove) 51, 61, 105
Calle Ocho Walk of Fame 15
Calle Ocho 6, **14–15**, 62, 63, 85, 86
Camille's 125
Cancun Grill (Miami Lakes) 61, 89
Cape Florida Lighthouse 73
Captain Tony's Saloon 124
Captiva Island Inn 131
Cardozo Hotel **11**, 147
Carl Fisher 45
Carlyle Hotel 73
Casa Casuarina 8
Casa Juancho 87
Casa Marina Resort (Key West) 148
Casa Panza 87, 89
Casino Records 88
Catch, The 125
Cathode Ray (Ft. Lauderdale) 52
Cauley Square Tea Room 109, 111
Cavalier Hotel **11**, 147
Cernuda Arte 43
Ceviche 61
Charles Deering Estate 107
Cheeca Lodge (Islamorada) 148
Cheesecake Factory 105
Chef Allen's 95
Cher 39
Chief Jim Billie 27
Children's Attractions 66–7
    Amelia Earhart Park 66
    Historical Museum of Southern Florida 67
    Hobie Beach 66
    Key West Aquarium 67
    Miami Children's Museum 90, 91
    Miami Metrozoo 66–7
    Miami Seaquarium 88
    Mini Amore (fashions for kids) 67
    Museum of Science and Planetarium 67
    Parrot Jungle Island 66
    Storytelling at the Biltmore 6
Chimichurri 61
China Grill 79

Chinese Village 18
Christy's 105
Churches
  Coral Gables Congregational
    Church **19**, 46, 99, 103
  Ermita de la Caridad Church
    (Coconut Grove) 48
  Gesú Church 84, 85
  Plymouth Congregational
    Church (Coconut Grove) **47**,
    101
  St. Paul's Episcopal Church
    (Key West) 117
Cigars 14
Clay Hotel and Youth Hostel
  (SoBe) 51, 152
Clewiston Inn 131
Climate 134
Club Tropigale 87
Cobblestone Antiques 110
Coconut Grove Playhouse
  38, 103
Coconut Grove Village 103
CocoWalk **50**, 100, 102
Coliseum 76
Collins Ave **9**, 73
Collins Avenue at 7th Street
  (SoBe) 75
Colonial Dining Room
  (Clewiston) 130
Colony Hotel **10**, 147
Colony Theater 38
Commodore Plaza 51, 102
Communications 141
Conch-blowing Contest 121
Conch chowder/fritters 61
Conch Republic Cigar Factory
  122
Conch Republic 26
Conch tour train 26, 121
Congregational Church (Coral
  Gables) 19, 103
Coral Castle 44, 48, 107
Coral Gables and Coconut
  Grove 98–105
Coral Gables 6, **18–19**
Coral Tree Inn (Key West) 153
Coral 119
Corkscrew Swamp 28–9
Crab House Seafood
  Restaurant 95
Crandon Beach **31**, 72
Crandon Park 72
Crane Point Hammock
  Museums & Nature Center
  118
Crobar 77
Crowne Plaza La Concha (Key
  West) 131
Cuba! Cuba! 122
Cuban American Heritage
  Festival 121
Cuban imports 15
Cubans 14–15
Cultura del Lobo 87

D
Dania Beach Historic Antique
  District 56
Dave Barry 39
Deco Architecture 12–13
Deco District 6, **10–13**, 46, 62
Deering Brothers, The **16–17**,
  45, 107
Deering, Charles 16–17, 45
Deering, James 16, 45
Delano Hotel 73, 147
Design District 92
D'Ester 110
Dewey, John 27
Diable En Deuil Botánica 94
Dinner Key 101
Divine Trash 94
Dixon, L. Murray 13
Dock at Crayton Cove (Naples)
  130
Dog racing 35
Dolphin Cove 115
Dolphin Mall 56
Dolphin Research Center 116
Domino Park 14, 15, 85
Doral Golf Resort and Spa 148
Double-crested cormorant 119
Doubletree Grand Key Resort
  149
Downtown and Little Havana
  82–89
Drives and walks 62–3
  Coco Village 63
  Deco district 63
  Everglades trails 63
  Key West Old Town 63
  Miami Beach to Key Biscayne
    62
  Miami to Key West 62
  Palm Beach 63
  Routes North 62
Dry Tortugas 121, 129
Dutch South African Village 19
Duval Beach Club 125
Duval House (Key West) 151
Duval Street (Key West) 26

E
Egrets 119
El Atlakat 89
El Crédito cigars **14**, 85, 88
El Crucero 89
Eleventh Street Diner 51, 79
Elian Gonzalez 49
Embassies and consulates 134
Emergency numbers 139
Emme Brazilian Sportswear 88
Endangered species 119
Environmental Circus 122
Ermita de la Caridad Church
  (Coconut Grove) 48
Escopazzo (SoBe) 60, 79
Española Way Market (SoBe) 57
Espanola Way **9**, 57

Estefan Enterprises 47
Estefan family 39, 49
Estefan, Gloria 15, 39
Eternal Flame 14
Everglades and Alligator Alley
  (I–75) 127
Everglades and Tamiami Trail
  (US41) 127
Everglades National Park 28
Everglades 7, **28–9**, 63, 127
Expertees Golf Shop 104
Exquisito 85, 89

F
Fairchild Tropical Garden **36**, 107
Fairmont Turnberry Isle
  (Aventura) 148
Fairvilla Megastore 123
Fakahatchee Strand 28–9
Falls Shopping Center 110
Fantasy Fest 40, 121
Festivals 40–41
  Annual Conch-blowing
    Contest 121
  Carnival Miami 40
  Coconut Grove Arts Festival
    40, 102
  Coconut Grove Arts Festival
    102
  Columbus Day Regatta 102
  Cuban American Heritage
    Festival 121
  Fantasy Fest (Key West) 40,
    121
  Festival of Haitian Art 102
  Goombay Celebration (Key
    West) 121
  Hemingway Days 121
  Hispanic Heritage Festival 41
  International Mango Festival
    41
  King Mango Strut 41
  Miami-Dade County Fair and
    Exposition 40
  Miami International Orchid
    Show 102
  Miami-Bahamas Goombay
    Festival 41, 102
  Old Island Days 121
  Seven-Mile Bridge Run 121
  South Beach Wine & Food 41
  Winter Party, White Party 40
Fisher Island Club 148
Flagler Museum (Palm Beach) 25
Flagler Street 84, 86
Flagler, Henry 26–7
Flamingo Gardens 37
Flamingo Hotel (Fort
  Lauderdale) 153
Flamingo 28–9
Floribbean Food 61
Florida Beach Hostel (Fort
  Lauderdale) 152
Florida Grand Opera 39
Florida International University
  Art Museum 109

Florida Keys National Marine Sanctuary 118
Florida Keys Wild Bird Rehabilitation Center 118
Florida Pioneer Village 19
Floyd's Youth Hostel (Fort Lauderdale) 152
Fontainebleau Resort & Towers 148
Football Player (Duane Hanson) 21
Football 35
Forge, The 50–51
Fort Lauderdale beaches 32
Fort Lauderdale-Hollywood International Airport 135
Fort Myers 128
Fort Zachary Taylor Historic State Park 26
Four Seasons (Palm Beach) 146
France, Robert F. 13
Freedom Tower 46, 83
French City Village 19
French Country Village 19
French Normandy Village 19
Fritz's Skate Shop 75
Front Porch Café 78
Frost, Robert 27
Fruit & Spice Park 36-7, 109

G

Gallery at the Kona Kai Resort 122
Garcia's Seafood Grille and Fish Market 89
Garden of Eden (Key West) 49, 117, 124
Gardens Hotel (Key West) 150
Gay and Lesbian Community Center of South Florida 52
Gay and Lesbian Community Center, Key West 123
Gay and Lesbian Spots
    Miami and Environs 52–3
    Key West 123
George Merrick 18–19, 45
Gesu Church 84–5
Giralda Café 105
Gold Coast Highway A1A 7, 24–5
Gold Coast Railroad Museum 108
Gold Coast, Treasure Coast, and A1A North 127-8
Goombay Celebration (Key West) 121
Graffiti (Key West) 123
Granada Gate (Coral Gables) 46
Grand Vin 122
Green Island Inn (Fort Lauderdale) 152
Green Parrot Bar 117, 124
Green Street Café 51, 102
Greynolds Park 93
Guadalajara 111
Guayacan 89
Gulfstream Park 35, 90, 93

Gumbo Limbo Nature Center (Boca Raton) 25
Gumbo Limbo tree 119
Gusman Center for the Performing Arts 39, 84, 87

H

Harbor Drive 72
Haulover Park Beach 30
Havana Shirt 88
Havana To Go 88
Hawk's Cay Resort (Duck Key) 148
Health and security information 139
Heart and Soul (Miami Beach) 75
Hemingway Days 121
Hemingway House (Key West) 27, 117
Hemingway, Ernest 27, 117
Henry M. Flagler 45
Herons 119
Hialeah Park 41
Hibiscus Hill 104
Hibiscus House (West Palm Beach) 131
Historic Homestead Museum 41
Historic Houses 44–5
    Charles Deering Estate 44, 107
    James Deering Estate 16–17, 107
    Merrick House (Coral Gables) 18–19, 44
    Opa-Locka 33, 91
    Stranahan House (Fort Lauderdale) 44
Hobie Island Beach 30–31
Hog's Breath Saloon 124
Hohauser, Henry 13
Hollywood Broadwalk 24, 51
Homestead Main Street 110
Horse racing 35
Hotel Astor (SoBe) 151
Hotel Intercontinental Miami 146
Hotel Leon (SoBe) 150
Hotel of South Beach 247
Hotel Place St. Michel (Coral Gables) 150
Hotel St. Augustine 153
Hotels
    Guesthouses and B&Bs 153
    Hostels and budget 151, 152
    Gay and Lesbian 153
    Lap of Luxury 146
    Resorts and Spas 131, 148
    SoBe 147
    Surfside retreats 149
Hotlines and helplines 144
Hurricane Andrew 45
Hyatt Regency Pier 66 (Fort Lauderdale) 131

I

Ice Hockey 35

IGFA Fishing Hall of Fame and Museum 24
Improv Comedy Club 102
In Touch (Key West) 123
Indian Key Historic State Park 115
Ingraham Building 46, 85
Inn on Fifth (Naples) 131
Intermix 94
International Villages (Merrick) 18–19, 99
Internet access 141
Island Colors 110
Island Houses for Men 153
Italian Village 19
It's A Take 94

J

Jackie Gleason Theater of the Performing Arts 38
Jackie Gleason 38–9
Jai Alai 35
James Hotel (SoBe) 151
Jay's Antiques and Collectibles 110
Jazid 77
Jeb Bush, Mrs. 49
Jerry's Famous Deli 73
Joe's Stone Crab 61, 79
Johnson, Don 39
John U. Lloyd Beach State Park (Dania) 24
Johnny Rockets 101, 102
José Martí Park 15, 86
Julia Tuttle 45
Jupiter Beach Resort 131

K

Kafka's Used Book Store & Cyber Café 75
Key Deer 119
Key Largo Hammocks Botanical State Park 118
Key Lime Bistro (Captiva) 130
Key Lime pie 61
Key West Aloe 122
Key West Art & History Museum 27
Key West Beaches 31
Key West Cemetery 27
Key West Hand Print 122
Key West Newspaper 138
Key West Old Town 26–7, 47
Key West Youth Hostel 152
Key West 7, 26–7, 117
Kichnell & Elliot 13
King Mango Strut 102
Kon Tiki Resort (Islamorada) 15
Kona Kai Resort (Key Largo) 149
KWEST (Key West) 123

L

La Carreta I 89
La Casa de los Trucos 85, 88
La Paloma 95
La Porteña 111

Labors of Hercules (Villa Vizcaya) 16
Lago Mar (Fort Lauderdale) 149
Lake Okeechobee 129
Language 134
Larios on the Beach 78
Laroche, the orchid thief 49
Las Olas Blvd (Fort Lauderdale) 25
Las Olas Café 24
La-Te-Da (Key West) 123
Le Café de Paris (Fort Lauderdale) 130
Le Neveu de Rameau (Frank Stella) 21
Lechon Asado 61
Leslie Hotel 11, 147
Liberty City 41
Lighthouse Museum (Key West) 27, 117
Lignumvitae Key Botanical State Park 118
Lincoln Road Mall 9, 50, 57
Lincoln Road Markets 57
Lincoln Theater 39
Lion Country Safari 36
Little Haiti 41, 91
Little Havana 6, 14–15, 86
Little Inn by the Sea (Lauderdale-by-the-Sea) 150
Little Managua (Calle Ocho) 41
Lively Arts 38–9
Loews Hotel 146
Long Key State Park 118
Los Pinareños Fruteria (Little Havana) 57, 88
Los Pinareños Fruteria 57, 85, 88
Los Ranchos of Bayside 87
Louie's Backyard 125
Lowe Art Museum 7, 20–21, 99
Loxahatchee National Wildlife Refuge 127
Lummus Park Beach 8, 30
Lyric Theater 41

M
Madiba 76
Madonna 39
Mahogony Hammock 29
Mallory Square (Key West) 26, 51
Malls and Shopping Centers 54–57
Mandarin Oriental 146
Mangia Mangia Pasta Café 125
Mangoes (Key West) 51, 117, 125
Mango's Tropical Café 51, 78
Mansion 58, 77
Manuel Artime Theater 87
Margaritaville 124
Marjory Stoneman Douglas Biscayne Nature Center (Crandon Park) 72
Marjory Stoneman Douglas 45
Mark's South Beach 60, 79
Marlin Hotel Bar 8

Marquesa Hotel (Key West) 150
Martí, Jose 27
Matheson Hammock Park Beach 31
Mayfair House 46
Media sources 138
Mediterranean Gallery 88
Mel Fisher's Maritime Heritage Society Museum (Key West) 27, 43, 117
Meller-Jensen, Barbara 49
Melting Pot, The 111
Mermaid & the Alligator (Key West) 150
Merrick House (Coral Gables) 103
Merrick Villages 18–19, 103
Merrick, George 6, 18–19
Metrobus 136
Metromover 86, 137
Metrorail and Metromover 137
Miami Beach and Key Biscayne 70–81
Miami Beach Travelers' Hostel (SoBe) 152
Miami Children's Museum 90, 91
Miami City Ballet 38–9
Miami Herald 138
Miami International Airport 135
Miami Metrozoo 107
Miami Metrozoo 36, 107
Miami News Times 138
Miami Performing Arts Center 38
Miami Seaquarium 72
Miami-Dade County Auditorium 39
Miami-Dade Cultural Center 83
Miccosukee Indian Village 41
Midori Gallery 104
Minar 94
Mini Oxygene 94
Miracle Mile 99, 103
Miracle Theater 38
Miss Cleo 49
Modernism Gallery 104
Modular Painting in Four Panels (Roy Lichtenstein) 21
Money 134, 141
Monkey Jungle 107
Monkey Jungle 36
Monty's Stone Crab Seafood House and Raw Bar (Coconut Grove) 61, 105
Morikami Museum and Japanese Gardens 37
Murals and Mosaics
    Bacardi Import Headquarters 47
    Bahama Village 47
    Coral Gables City Hall 47
    Little Havana 14-15, 47
    Miami Beach Post Office 47
    Office Building (South Beach) 47
    Society of the Four Arts (Palm Beach) 47
    The Netherland 47

Murals and Mosaics (cont.)
    Wyland Whaling Walls (Key West) 47
Museum of Contemporary Art (Miami) 92
Museum of Natural History of the Florida Keys 116
Museums and Monuments
    Ah-Tah-Thi-Ki Museum 29, 43
    AIDS Memorial (Key West) 123
    Ancient Spanish Monastery 44, 91
    Barnacle House, The 44, 100
    Bass Museum of Art 42, 71
    Brigade 2506 Memorial 14, 44
    Coral Castle 44, 108
    Coral Gables Merrick House 18–19, 44
    Cuban Museum of the Americas 15, 42
    Flagler Museum (Palm Beach) 25
    Florida International University Art Museum 109
    Gold Coast Railroad Museum 108
    Graves Museum of Archaeology and Natural History (Dania) 24
    Historic Homestead Museum 41
    Historical Museum of Southern Florida 42-3
    Holocaust Memorial 44
    Jewish Museum of Florida 43
    Key West Art & History Museum 27
    Lighthouse Museum 117
    Lowe Art Museum 7, 20–21, 42
    Maritime Museum of the Florida Keys 43, 115
    Mel Fisher's maritime Museum (Key West) 27
    Miami Art Museum 42
    Miami Children's Museum 90, 91
    Museum of Contemporary Art (Miami) 92
    Museum of Natural History of the Florida Keys 116
    Villa Vizcaya 6, 16–17, 44
    Wolfsonian 7, 22–3, 42
    Wreckers' Museum (Key West) 117
    Norton Museum of Art (Palm Beach) 25
Mynt 59, 77

N
Nancy's Secret Garden (Key West) 37, 49
Naples 128
Nash Hotel 147
National Hotel 147
National Key Deer Refuge 118

Nature Preserves 118
  see also State and national
  parks
Neil, Freddie 27
Nelson, Henry O. 13
News Café 8, 51, 78
Nightlife
  Miami 58–59
  SoBe 76–77
  Keys 124
Noodles Panini 24
Norman's Restaurant (Coral
  Gables) 60, 105
North of Downtown 90–97
Norton Museum of Art (Palm
  Beach) 25

O
Oasis Guesthouse (Key West) 153
O'Donnell, Rosie 39, 49
Ocean Drive 8, 50
Ocean Surf Hotel 149
Oceanfront Auditorium 10
Oka-Locka/Hialeah Flea Market
  57
Old City Hall 9
Old Cuba Collection 88
Old Island Days 121
Old Lisbon 89
Old Town Ghost Walk (Key
  West) 121
Old Town Resorts (Key West) 149
One Duval 125
Opa-Locka 45, 48, 90–91
Opium Garden 77
Out of Africa 104
Overton Historic Village 41

P
Pacific Time (SoBe) 60, 79
Palm Beach 25, 63
Palm Produce Resortwear 104
Palm trees 119
Pancoast, Russell 13
Paninoteca 51
Paquito's Mexican Restaurant
  93, 95
Park Central 10, 147
Parking 8, 145
Parks, gardens, and zoos 36–7
Parrot Jungle Island 36, 71
Passports and visas 134
Peacock Park (Coconut Grove)
  101
Pearl's Rainbow (Key West) 153
Pelican Café 78
Pennekamp Coral Reef State
  Park 115, 118
Penrod's Complex 59, 77
Peppers of Key West 122
Perkey's Bat Tower (Sugarloaf
  Key) 49
Peter Miller Hotel (SoBe) 152
P. F. Chang's China Bistro 95
Pier House & Caribbean Spa
  (Key West) 146

Pigeon Key 116–117
Pineapple Point (Fort
  Lauderdale) 153
Plaza de la Cubanidad 15
Plymouth Congregational
  Church (Coconut Grove) 47
Polevitsky, Igor 13
Polo 35
Presidential election 2000
  49
Public House (South Beach) 75

R
Radio and television 138
Raleigh Hotel 147
Red Fish Grill 111
Red Reef Park (Boca Raton) 33,
  37
Restaurant Place St. Michel 105
Restaurants
  Coral Gables and Coconut
    Grove 105, 111
  Fort Lauderdale 130
  Keys, The 125
  Little Havana 89
  Miami 60–61
  North of Downtown 95
  SoBe 78–79
  South of Coconut Grove 111
  Top Ten restaurants 60–61
Rex (Deborah Butterfield) 21
Rick's Blue Heaven 26, 125
Rick's Dirty Harry's 124
Ricky Martin 39, 50
Ritz Carlton
  Key Biscayne 148
  South Beach 149
Ritz Plaza 73
Rod and Gun Club and Lodge
  (Everglades) 130–31
Romantic Spots 64–5
  Ancient Spanish Monastery
    Cloister & Gardens 64
  Coral Castle 65
  Fairchild Tropical Garden 64
  Hotel Place St. Michel 65
  Mallory Square (Key West) 65
  Morikami Japanese Gardens
    65
  Red Fish Grill 65, 111
  Tantra Restaurant 65
  Venetian Pool 64
  Villa Vizcaya Gardens 63
Royal Palms Resort (Fort
  Lauderdale) 153
Rules of the road 137

S
St. Augustine, Hotel 153
St. Moritz Hotel 73
St. Paul's Episcopal Church
  (Key West) 117
San Carlos Opera House 117
Sanibel and Captiva Islands 129
Sanibel Harbour Resort and
  Spa 131

Santeria and Vodou Botánicas
  15, 48
Sawgrass Mills Mall 56
Score 76
Sea Lord (Fort Lauderdale) 150
Sea turtles 119
Seminole and Native American
  artworks 21
Senior and disabled travelers
  143
Seven-Mile Bridge Run 121
Seven-Mile Bridge 26
Seybold Building 56
Shark Valley 28
Shelborne Resort (SoBe) 149
Sheraton Bal Harbour Resort
  146
Shopping
  Coral Gables and Coconut
    Grove 104, 110
  The Keys 44, 122, 123
  Key West 122
  Little Havana 88, 94
  Miami 54, 56
  Miami Beach 75
  North of Downtown 94
  South of Coconut Grove 110
Shula's Steak House 111
Side Trips 126–131
Sidewalk Cafés 78
Sinclair's Ocean Grill (Jupiter)
  130
Skislewicz, Anton 13
Sloppy Joe's Bar 117, 124
Snorkeling and Diving 32–3
SoBe 6, 8–9, 57
SoBe and the Deco District 71
SoBe Clubs 76–7
SoBe Streetlife 62
SoBe You 153
South Beach lifeguard huts 11,
  48
South Beach Local 137
South Beach Plaza Villas 150
South of Coconut Grove
  106–113
South Pointe Park Beach 30
Southwinds Motel (Key West)
  151
Soyka 95
Special tours and events in the
  Keys 121
Spectator sports 35
Sports 34–5
  Bicycling 35, 74, 120
  Boating and Kayaking 34, 120
  Dolphin swims 34, 115–16
  Fishing 35, 74, 120
  Golf 35, 74, 120
  In-line skating 34, 75
  Jet-skiing, parasailing, and
    water-skiing 34, 74, 120
  Kite-flying 74
  Snorkeling and diving 32–3,
    120
  Sports in the Keys 120

Sports (cont.)
Swimming 74, 120
Tennis 35, 74, 120
Volleyball 34, 74
Windsurfing and surfing 34, 74, 120
Workouts 74
Square Shopping Center (Key Biscayne) 75
State and national parks
Bahia Honda State Park **31**, 117, 118
Bill Baggs Cape Florida 31
Biscayne National Underwater Park 32
Crane Point Hammock Museums & Nature Center 118
Dolphin Cove 115
Dolphin Research Center 116
Dry Tortugas National Park 32, 129
Florida Keys National Marine Sanctuary 118
Florida Keys Wild Bird Rehabilitation Center 118
Fort Zachary Taylor Historic State Park 26
Indian Key Historic State Park 116
John Pennekamp Coral Reef State Park 32, 115, 118
Key Biscayne Parks 31, **32**, 72-3
Key Largo Hammocks Botanical State Park 118
Lignumvitae Key Botanical State Park 118
John U. Lloyd Beach State Park 24
Looe Key National Marine Sanctuary 32
Long Key State Park 118
Loxahatchee National Wildlife Refuge 127
Maritime Museum of the Florida Keys 115
Museum of Natural History of the Florida Keys 116
National Key Deer Refuge 118
Pigeon Key 116–117
Red Reef Park (Boca Raton) 33
Theater of the Sea 115
Windley Key Fossil Reef State Geological Site 118
Stiltsville (Key Biscayne) 49
Stock-car racing 35
Streamline Moderne Diner 22
Streets of Mayfair Mall (Coconut Grove) 101, 104
Studio 76
Sunny Isles Beach 30
SuperShuttle 135
Sushi Maki 111

Swamp Water Café (Everglades) 28, 130
Swap Shop (Fort Lauderdale) 57
Swartburg, Robert 13

T
Tantra 59, 65, 77
Tamiami Trail (US 41) 28
Tap Tap (SoBe) 60, 79
Teatro de Bellas Artes 87
Teatro Ocho 87
Tennis 35
Terrace at the Tides 50, 78
The Breakers (Palm Beach) 25
The Brigade 14
The Broadwalk (Fort Lauderdale) 24
The Gilded Hand 104
The Keys 114–135
The Wrestler 22-3
Theater of the Sea 115
Things to avoid 140
Tide Vacation Apartments (Hollywood Beach) 151
Tides Hotel 147
Titanic Brewing Company 20, 105
Tito Puente, Jr. 39
Today's Collectibles 110
Top Lounge 124
Tourist information 135, 142, 145
Tours 134, 137
Trattoria Sole 111
Treasure Village 122
Tropical Chinese 111
Tropical Deco 12–13
Tropical drinks 59
Tropics Hotel and Hostel (SoBe) 152
Truman, Harry S. 27
Trump International Sonesta Beach Resort 148
Twist 76
Two Chefs 111

U
Unicorn Creations 110
Upscale Shopping 54–5
Urban Garden 94
US Federal Courthouse 83

V
Van Dyke Café 51, 78
Venetian Pool **18–19**, 64, 99, 103
Venevision 87
Veranda (Fort Myers) 130
Versace, Gianni 8, 49
Versailles Cuban Restaurant **14–15**, 60–61, 89
Vierge Miracle & Botánica Saint Philippe 94
Villa Paradiso (SoBe) 150
Villa Vizcaya 6, **16–17**, 44, 100, 103

Virginia Key Beach 30–31

W
Waldorf Towers 10, 147
Walks, drives, historic sites
Coral Gables and Coconut Grove 101, 102
Deco District (Miami Beach) 72
Downtown and Little Havana 85–86
The Keys 121
Key West 117
Miami 62–63
Washington Ave 9
Wet Willie's 78
White House Shop 104
White ibis 119
Williams, Tennessee 27
Windjammer Resort and Beach Club (Lauderdale-by-the-Sea) 149
Windley Key Fossil Reef State Geological Site 118
Wings Over Miami 108
Wolfie Cohen's Rascal House 95
Wolfson, Mitchell Jr. 22
Wolfsonian Museum 7, **22-3**
Woodlawn Cemetery 15
World Erotic Art Museum 42
Worth Avenue (Palm Beach) 25
Wreckers' Museum 117
Wyndham Grand Bay Hotel 146

Y
Yuca 79
Yucca/Plantain chips 61

Acknowledgements

The Author
Jeffrey Kennedy is a freelance travel writer who divides his time between the Iberian Peninsula and the USA.

Produced by BLUE ISLAND PUBLISHING
Editorial Director Rosalyn Thiro
Art Director Stephen Bere
Associate Editor Michael Ellis
Designer Lee Redmond
Picture Research Ellen Root
Research Assistance Amaia Allende
Factcheck, Index Mary Sutherland
Main Photographer Peter Wilson
Additional Photography Max Alexander, Dave King, Neil Mersh, Paolo Pulga, Clive Streeter, Stephen Whitehorn, Linda Whitwam
Cartography Encompass Graphics

AT DORLING KINDERSLEY
Series Publisher Douglas Amrine
Publishing Managers Fay Franklin, Jane Ewart
Senior Art Editor Marisa Renzullo
Cartographic Editor Caspar Morris
DTP Jason Little, Conrad van Dyk
Production Melanie Dowland
Editorial and Additional Contributors
Mark Bailey, Naftali Farber, Jo Gardner, Esther Labi, Sam Merrell, Mani Ramaswamy, Collette Sadler, Phyllis and Arvin Steinberg, Ros Walford
Picture Credits
Dorling Kindersley would like to thank all the many establishments covered in this book for their assistance and kind permission for the producers to take photographs.

Placement Key: t–top; tl–top left; tr–top right; tc–top center; tcl–top center left; c–center; cr–center right; b–bottom; bl–bottom left; br–bottom right.

AFP: 49br; THE ART OF SHAVING: 94br; CARNAVAL MIAMI: 40b; CAULEY SQUARE HISTORIC VILLAGE: 110tl, 110tr; COCONUT GROVE ARTS FESTIVAL: 40tl; CORBIS: 39cr; Tony Arruza 112-3; Bettmann 39tr; Mitchell Gerber 49tr; Reuters/Fred Prouser 39br;

EVERGLADES NATIONAL PARK: 119tl; FLORIDA GRAND OPERA: Photo Debra Hesser 38tr; FLORIDA KEYS NEWS BUREAU: Andy Newman 41tl; TOM J FRANKS: 40c; BARBARA GILLMAN GALLERY: 43br; GREATER MIAMI CONVENTION AND VISITORS BUREAU: 8–9, 14cr, 28t, 35l all, 38c, 64c, 66c, 70tcl, 72t, 74tl, 74tl, 115b, 136tl; GULFSTREAM PARK RACETRACK: 90tr; HISPANIC HERITAGE FESTIVAL: 41bl; HISTORICAL MUSEUM OF SOUTHERN FLORIDA: 42tr; INTERMIX: 90tl; Monte Verde dress by Catherine Malandrino 90c; INTERNATIONAL MANGO FESTIVAL: Suzanne Kores 40tr; LINCOLN THEATER: 38tc; LOS RANCHOS: 87tl; LOWE ART MUSEUM, UNIVERSITY OF MIAMI: 20t/20b/21 all, 21b (c) Duane Hanson/ VAGA, New York and DACS, London 2002, 42tl; MANGOES: Havana Inc. 125tl; MARQUESA HOTEL: Dan Forer 150tr; MIAMI-DADE COUNTY FAIR AND EXPOSITION: 40tc; MIAMI DESIGN DISTRICT: Owner: Craig Robins; Artists: Rosario Marquardt and Roberto Behar *Mural Detail, Buick Building* 46tc; MORIKAMI MUSEUM FLORIDA: 36tr; NHPA: Trevor McDonald 32b; Tom & Therisa Stack 33t; STUART NEWMAN ASSOCIATES: 121tr; NORTON MUSEUM OF ART: 42br; THE OPIUM GROUP: 77t; Simon Hare Photography 58br; PALM BEACH COUNTY CONVENTION AND VISITORS BUREAU: 32tl; PENROD'S COMPLEX: 58tr, 59tl; PICTURES COLOUR LIBRARY: 128b, 129b; THE RITZ-CARLTON KEY BISCAYNE: 148tl; SOUTH BEACH GAY MEN'S CHORUS: Roberto Ferreira 38tl; TARA, Ink.: Seth Browarnik 58tl,70tr, 77tc; THEATER OF THE SEA: 116tr; TWIST: Valentino Eriksen 76tr; WALGREENS: IDT 141tr; WOLFSONIAN-FLORIDA INTERNATIONAL UNIVERSITY: 7tr, 22r, 22b, 22l, 23c, 23b, 23t, 42tc, 42c.

All other images are © Dorling Kindersley. For more information see www.dkimages.com

Cartography Credits
Martin Darlison (Encompass Graphics Ltd)

Special Editions of DK Travel Guides

DK Travel Guides can be purchased in bulk quantities at discounted prices for use in promotions or as premiums. We are also able to offer special editions and personalized jackets, corporate imprints, and excerpts from all of our books, tailored specifically to meet your own needs.

To find out more, please contact:

(in the United States) **SpecialSales@dk.com**

(in the UK) **Sarah.Burgess@dk.com**

(in Canada) DK Special Sales at **general@tourmaline.ca**

(in Australia) **business.development @pearson.com.au**